Why Smart People Lose a Fortune

5 Steps to Restoring Your Wealth and Sanity

Dear Dr Chung, Aurora & Ed,

Best Wishes & Health!

I appreciate your trust & friendship.

Praise for
Why Smart People Lose a Fortune

"*Why Smart People Lose a Fortune* takes **a critical look at the truth behind why so many lose so much when it comes to investing.** Frankle's honest approach shows true concern for his readers and their level of financial success."

ANTHONY ROBBINS
Best-selling author of *Awaken the Giant Within* and *Unlimited Power*

"It makes sense to invest when the market shows strength and to get out of the market when it shows weakness. Frankle shows investors how to do just that—and stop losing their shirts. **I wish this book had been around a long time ago.**"

JOHN ASSARAF
Best-selling author of *The Street Kid's Guide to Having It All*

"This book will open any investor's eyes to the hidden pitfalls of investing in today's chaotic market. The author, Neal Frankle, a financial advisor, destroys common misperceptions about investing and shows a way all investors can avoid the biggest common mistakes. In an easy-to-read style, the author takes the reader on a **journey toward investment nirvana—an investment portfolio that never disappoints.**"

STEVE MOELLER
President, American Business Vision, LLC

"The book provides a solution to every investor's dilemma: how to protect principal in down markets and how to grow in up markets. **This book is an essential tool for those who are serious about reaching their financial goals and who want a strategy that will help them sleep soundly at night.** Don't just buy this book; *use it.*"
 NATHAN MERSEREAU, Certified Financial Planner®

"Frankle **debunks the myths of buy and hold and asset allocation.** He protects investors from the illusions and deceptions of Wall Street, stock brokers, and mutual funds."
 DICK SANDNES, President, Mr. Stax Incorporated
 An International House of Pancakes Management Company

"Frankle does a great job and gets down to business. His message is clear and sharp. **If you follow these simple rules, you will not only grow your money, you'll also have greater peace of mind.**"
 E. MARTIN VON KANEL, Certified Financial Planner®,
 Certified Senior Advisor

"A direct, no-nonsense approach that deciphers the mysteries surrounding investing and personal finance . . . *Why Smart People Lose a Fortune* is refreshingly gimmick-free and based on Frankle's solid experience."
 ADAM ARKIN, Actor, Director

Why Smart People Lose a Fortune

5 Steps to Restoring Your Wealth and Sanity

NEAL FRANKLE
CERTIFIED FINANCIAL PLANNER®

JUST WRITE BOOKS
LOS ANGELES

WHY SMART PEOPLE LOSE A FORTUNE. Copyright © 2004 by Neal Frankle. All rights reserved. No part of this publication may be reproduced, stored in a retrieval system, or transmitted in any form or by any means (electronic, mechanical, photocopying, recording, or otherwise) without the written permission of the author. For information, contact Wealth Resources Group, 5855 Canyon Blvd., Suite 420, Woodland Hills, California, 91367.

Reference is made throughout this book to the *Investor's Business Daily* and CAN SLIM™, which is an investment method created by William O'Neil. Readers should not take this to mean that the investment method presented here is an example of CAN SLIM or that the method presented here is endorsed by Mr. O'Neil or the *Investor's Business Daily*. There is no connection, association, sponsorship, and/or affiliation between *Investor's Business Daily*, their products and services, and this book.

Reference is also made to *NoLoad Fund*X*, an investment newsletter published by the DAL Investment Company. The method presented in this book is neither an example of *NoLoad Fund*X* nor is it endorsed by the DAL Company. There is no connection, association, sponsorship, and/or affiliation between *NoLoad Fund*X* or DAL, their products and services, and this book.

Edited by Just Write Literary & Editorial Partners, JustWriteNow.com
Designed and produced by Robert Mott & Associates, Mottopia.com

ISBN: 0-9749830-1-2

This publication is designed to provide accurate, useful, and authoritative information in regard to the subject matter covered. It is sold with the understanding that the publisher is not engaged in rendering legal, accounting, or other professional service. Laws vary from state to state, and if legal or expert assistance is required, the services of a competent professional person should be sought. The author and publisher specifically disclaim any responsibility for liability, loss, or risk, personal or otherwise, that is incurred as a consequence, directly or indirectly, of the use and application of any of the contents of this book.

To Rena and Albert Klein, my family.

To my daughters Rinat, Mor, and Maya, my treasures.

To my wife, Mimi, my light.

Acknowledgments

I could never have completed this project without the unselfish support I received from all corners of my life. This book is a result of the gifts I have received throughout my life more than it is a result of anything I have done.

Thank you, Diane Cairnes, for reminding me what I do for a living and for a great deal of help and encouragement in the early stages of this project. I also express my gratitude to Nancy Sobel, for helping me see that wealth is measured by what I can give rather than what I have, and to Sean Mc Farland, the guy with the best fastball in town. Thanks to personal friends Adam, Tom, Danny, Ian, and John, a great band of brothers. Al and Rena Klein and their children, Michael, Lisa, Lori, Karen, Amy, Judy, Gerri and Rachael, gave me light, hope, and love. Thank you! I owe you everything.

Thanks also to Ron Ogulnick, Larry Klein, Neri Bukspan, Don Salka, Naomi Cohen, Chuck Gold, Terry Oberman, Daryl Groves, Keith Smuckler, Arthur Wells, Steve Karr, and Uzi Gal for their support and encouragement.

Kudos to Karen Risch and the entire staff of Just Write for your expertise, skill, and sense of humor.

Special appreciation to Steve Moeller and Bill Bachrach: I would never have started this project without you.

Endless praise to Karrie Ghezzi for being the best client service manager on the planet.

Thanks Mimi, Rinat, Mor, and Maya for the continuous stream of love, support, and encouragement during the long hours I spent on this project.

Finally, thank you to Avraham Amar for sharing so much with me. You were the greatest example of class, respect, honesty, and humility I can ever hope to encounter.

How to Get Your FREE Bonuses

You receive a
Complete Course in Market-sensitive Investing
With the purchase of this book!

You are entitled to receive, *free of charge,* **three bonus gifts just for buying this book:** an audio tutorial in using this investment method and two special reports,
7 Ways You Can Slash Your Tax and *3 Ways To Retire 10 Years Early—Or Stay Retired 30 Years Longer.*
Please visit our website to download them for free:

http://www.NealFrankle.com/get_bonuses.html

Contents

Introduction 1

1. **Know Yourself**
   Make Sure Your Values Drive Your Decisions 11
2. **Face Facts**
   Base Your Decisions on How the Market Really Works 23
3. **Pay Attention**
   Listen to the Market, Not the Media 45
4. **Take Action**
   Generate Income with Your Investments 69
5. **Be Selective**
   Know How Advisers Work (You Over) 91
6. **Get Real**
   Recognize Asset Allocation for What It Truly Is (And Is Not) ..115
7. **Choose Carefully**
   *Buck the Wall Street System: Select Investments
   That Are Right for You* 129
8. **Watch Out**
   Develop Your Market Sensitivity 151
9. **Begin Now**
   Take 5 Steps to Market-Sensitive Investing 163
10. **Invest Wisely**
    Use This Method to Succeed with the Market 173

Afterword 181

Appendixes:
A. Selected Bibliography and Suggested Reading 183
B. How Bonds Work 185
C. How Equities Investments Work 191
D. How Mutual Funds Work 195

About the Author 203

Introduction

"Learn to listen.
Opportunity sometimes knocks very softly."
H. JACKSON BROWN, JR., Life's Little Instruction Book

I know you. You're a smart person. You've successfully navigated almost every aspect of your life. You own a nice home and reliable cars. You pay your bills on time. You're organized and intelligent, taking care of yourself and your family.

I've known you for the past 18 years.

You are (or were, if you're retired) an engineer, a manager, a teacher, an office manager or administrator, a scientist, a small business owner, an agent, or a doctor. You do your job well. You've been in your profession for many years, you've worked hard, and you've advanced.

Sit back. Think about everything you've accomplished—it's impressive. Obviously, you're not a dummy.

Then why do you lose money in the stock market?

You listen to what the Wall Street experts tell you. You make sensible and sound decisions based on their advice, but you still end up losing money. It's as if no one is telling you the *real* rules of the game.

While everything else in your life seems to be working pretty smoothly, the market plunges deeper and deeper into the abyss, your account keeps shrinking, and all you hear from your adviser is "buy and hold." Of course, your gut tells you your adviser should be able to come up with something better than that. You feel something is terribly wrong. You do what your adviser suggests—

albeit grudgingly—because that person is supposed to be the "expert."

You realize the professionals know more than you do, so you don't understand why your broker doesn't protect you. You invest in mutual funds and don't understand how they work or why the fund manager doesn't do anything to stop the bleeding, either.

You don't have any idea whom you can trust for financial advice or where to find that trustworthy person—if one exists anywhere. Do you even need a financial adviser? Why pay someone who doesn't add value?

Sometimes things go well, but when they don't, you question whether you should even invest at all. How can you protect yourself? Maybe you give up on the stock market altogether. It sounds like a good plan when you turn on the television and see corporate scandals starring the companies in which you've invested your life savings. As you watch guys like Dennis Kozlowski (ex-CEO of Tyco) and Samuel Waksal (founder of ImClone) indicted for fraud, insider trading, or tax evasion, no wonder you feel ripped off.

You should know you're not alone: Individual investors aren't the only people hurt by the "professionals." In 2002, state pension funds blamed Wall Street asset managers for more than $150 billion in losses—and that was on top of huge losses in the prior two years. CalPERS, California's $133 billion pension fund, fired Goldman Sachs and Merrill Lynch in 2002. Maryland, Massachusetts, and Illinois all fired from one to six of their "professional" advisers.

Before we get too much further, I should disclose that I'm a financial adviser, and I've been employed as one since 1984. But the good news is I'm not asking you to have blind faith in what I'm about to share with you. I only ask you not to consider me one of "them" until you hear me out.

INTRODUCTION

As a young man, I felt bamboozled by the financial services industry, too. At the age of 17 I received a small life insurance boon from my parents' policy. I knew I had to make this money work because I didn't have any other financial support.

I explained to my father's broker that I needed to invest this money to pay for my college education.

He suggested I buy bonds. He explained how they worked and what I could expect. He told me I'd receive a nice fat interest check every six months, and at the maturity of the bonds, I'd get my investment back. I liked what I heard, so everything was set up and I was happy.

But then the broker kept calling me. He suggested that I sell the bonds and buy something else.

I didn't understand this at all.

If the bonds were a good investment for my purposes six months ago, why did they need to be sold now? My needs hadn't changed, nor had the safety of the investments.

He kept calling. He kept urging me to sell the bonds and buy something else.

I didn't know anything about commissions at the time, but I did know enough to smell a skunk.

Something inside told me to hold the bonds and dump the broker—and that's exactly what I did. I didn't know why, but my intuition was strong. And it was right. I held the bonds through college and then some. They paid 14 percent and never missed a payment.

"In the middle of difficulty lies opportunity."
ALBERT EINSTEIN, Physicist

How I Developed My "Safety Net" Investment Method

I mentioned earlier that I've been employed as a financial adviser since 1984. I didn't say that I've *been* a financial adviser since 1984 because for the first few years, I had no idea what I was doing—I certainly was no financial adviser.

I especially remember my first few months at work. My responsibility was to help people make smart decisions about their money. This was a noble goal; the only problem was I had no experience and I had no understanding of how to do what I was supposed to do. But I had to make a living, so I studied the "elders." I had to rely on other people's experiences and learn from them. My teachers were mainly mutual fund representatives, the wholesalers whose job it was to get every broker on the planet to sell their products.

From these elders of finance, I learned the great money mantras: *Buy and hold. Think long term. Use asset allocation. Stay invested in equities all the time. Periods of market declines are short and upturns are longer—stay in, ride it out!* (Since then I've learned that all of these sayings are a bunch of baloney, but I'll explain that in detail later in the book.)

Parroting my elders worked. The clients did business with me. They made money. I made a living. It was a happy life! For the next 16 years, I held onto these profitable maxims and never wavered.

Lucky for both me and my clients, I continued my investment education. Along the way, I read William O'Neil's book, *How to Make Money in Stocks: A Winning System in Good Times or Bad*, which introduced me to his CAN SLIM™ investment system, a method to evaluate the strength of the market, the industry, and the stock before making an investment.[1] (Later in this book, you'll learn more about how I've adapted this method.) I fell in love with CAN SLIM

INTRODUCTION

and began using it immediately with my own money and with a select few clients who were willing to do something different.

Accompanied by thousands of investors who wanted to minimize risk and maximize gain with their investments by "taking the market's temperature," the principles of CAN SLIM gave me the tools to help clients avoid catastrophic mistakes.[2] It also helped me take advantage of good markets when they presented themselves. More important, it helped me recognize two distinct situations: When to be in the market and when to be out.

> *Important disclosure: Like anything else, my investment method is not perfect. There are no guarantees that using such techniques will enhance investment performance. Any time people invest, they take the risk of losing money.*

With these models, I based my recommendations on something of substance, rather than on my gut feeling about what the future might or might not hold. Using tools to take the market's temperature before investing replaced relying on the truisms of yesteryear for my clients who invested in stocks.

However, at the time I adopted this strategy, the majority of my clients still preferred mutual funds, and O'Neil didn't provide anything new for those clients. So for those investors, I simply relied on what I'd learned as a young Jedi: *Buy and hold. Think long term.*

---

[1] CAN SLIM is an acronym for those qualities a stock should have in order to be a buy candidate according to O'Neil. For a thorough discussion of this, see William J. O'Neil, *How to Make Money in Stocks* (New York: McGraw-Hill, 2002). The last letter in CAN SLIM is M, and it stands for Market Direction. O'Neil provides tools to determine the overall health of the market; for purposes of this book, I use those tools only. The method described later in this book is not an application of CAN SLIM.

[2] William J. O'Neil, *How to Make Money in Stocks*, 3rd ed.: "Based on surveys, we estimate up to 50,000 of IBD's experienced readers have made and nailed down significant gains during the 1990s. They did this by . . . paying close attention to IBD's 'Big Picture' daily market column . . . one of the rare sources that clearly told readers it was time to sell and raise cash in March and April 2000 and again in September 2000."

Use asset allocation. Stay invested in equities all the time. Down periods in the market are short and upturns are longer—stay in, ride it out! It worked. Life was good for everyone.

Then came the millennium.

In March 2000, as I measured the health of the overall market, it was clearly time to get out of individual stocks. I did so. I sold all my clients' stocks just before the market started its long and windy road downhill.

As wonderful as this sounds, I must painfully point out that 98 percent of the money I managed for clients was in funds—and they were following the buy-and-hold strategy.

So, while I did sell all the individual stocks, I held onto my mutual funds. If you had mutual funds yourself during this period, and you were holding, you know what came next.

Damn the Torpedoes

Most people resist change, and I was no exception. In March 2000, like it or not, things started changing in the investment world. I didn't recognize it, and I certainly didn't want to accept it.

You probably know that 2000 was the start of a very painful time in the equity markets. Prior to this stock market meltdown, many investors were fully invested in technology stocks. It's probably more accurate to say people were throwing money at tech stocks. Tech stocks were the only ones going up in price in any meaningful way at the time, and many were growing by leaps and bounds daily.

Technology was all anyone wanted to own until early 2000. But from March through December 2000, tech investors saw something they never thought possible: losses. Big losses.

In fact, from March through December of that year, the NASDAQ lost close to 50 percent of its value. If you had $500,000 invested in March 2000, you could have seen your account shrivel to $250,000 by the end of the year. That had to hurt!

INTRODUCTION

Even though I sold all my clients' individual stocks and refused to buy anything else, I continued to counsel my mutual-fund clients to hold. When fund clients called to ask what I was doing to protect them from the awful market, I told them I was protecting them by not paying attention to the market at all. I informed clients that riding it out was the smartest thing to do—and in my heart of hearts, I believed this to be true. Buy and hold was all I knew when it came to mutual funds. It was all anyone knew.

At first, my clients and I agreed that it made perfect sense not to sell the funds. The only problem was, the market ferociously chewed up their accounts every day.

We comforted one another. We'd been down this road before. The market always came back in a few months, didn't it? This was sure to be like all those times before, right?

Wrong. Things change.

This time the market didn't come back. As you know, it just kept going down. Clients started complaining. This bothered me. After all, didn't they know I was doing them the biggest favor of their lives? *Stocks for the long haul!* I chanted the mantras for them on cue, but—can you believe this?—they still complained about losing money. What nerve!

A few clients left me. Shortly before one of my better clients closed her accounts, she asked me a pivotal question: "When do we take yes for an answer and when do we take no for an answer?" In essence, she was asking me, *When do we start listening to what the market is telling us and stop telling the market what it ought to be doing?*

I thought long and hard about that question.

For stocks, I already had the answer. We'd implemented a method that did take yes for an answer and also took no for an answer—the CAN SLIM strategy. But for mutual funds, I had no answer—just a few well-rehearsed clichés.

I realized that these beliefs had led to clients losing too much money.

Everything I Need to Know I Learned from My Clients

Most folks understand that investing in the market means they have the possibility of losing money at some time or another—but at this point, the buy-and-hold method meant losing too much. I started to understand my clients much better. Rather than try to reeducate them, I started paying attention to clients and learning from them.

I began to understand that my job isn't to recite mantras, but actually to help people achieve their financial goals. The responsibility of a financial adviser is to protect clients against financial catastrophes, take advantage of the right opportunities and, sometimes, protect clients from themselves.

This was the turning point for me. While I had a great method to protect clients' money when they invested in individual stock positions, I needed to protect fund investors as well. I spent the next 18 months developing a way to do just that. I adapted the tools in CAN SLIM that measure market strength, plus other successful investment methods, to help make better investments in mutual funds, index funds, and exchange-traded funds (ETFs).

I call this my safety net strategy. I looked at many ways to apply this safety net before finalizing it. In this book, I'll show you how to apply this method for yourself. You don't have to be an investment genius to use it, but it will require a little work and practice. I think you'll find the results well worth the effort.

Time for the Truth

I've made many mistakes. I lost money for my clients and myself, and I didn't like it at all. I knew that if I couldn't find a way to actually help clients, I'd better find a new business.

INTRODUCTION

Throughout this book, I do my best to address the greatest concern of investors—how to stop worrying about their money. I pull back the curtains and show you the real wizards of Wall Street—and you'll see they are neither so big nor all-powerful. They don't know that much, and often they don't have your interests in mind.

Along the way, I explain the stock market and different types of financial advisers and investments. I show you exactly why you lose money and give you a set of rules to protect yourself. We look at how these rules operate, and we look at some of your misconceptions about money, advisers, investments, and methods. This will help you understand why you lose so much money in the market. Finally, I share a few tools that I use that can help you make better investment decisions. And along the way, I treat you like you deserve to be treated—as an intelligent adult.

As I'm sure you've gathered by now, I am highly critical of the conventional investment "wisdom." I demonstrate that the commonly held investment beliefs of investors, financial advisers, the media, and fund and brokerage companies cost you a fortune. I also show that you have good alternatives to these disastrous strategies.

Most investment advisers shy away from criticizing colleagues, let alone the industry itself. It isn't considered cricket. The good news for you is that I don't know how to play cricket, and I'm not interested in learning.

This book would have no value to you if I couldn't be very clear and direct about what I see as significant failures on the part of the mutual fund and brokerage industry. I feel that the financial industry's main objective should be to serve clients first and make profits second. When this gets mixed up, you suffer.

Many people in this industry are honest and interested in helping clients. But most professionals in this industry don't have the tools to help their clients, nor is their business set up to maximize benefits to you, the client.

I'm not trying to say that I'm above my peers in any way. I've made all the mistakes detailed in this book, and then some. It's simply time for money to do its job, to create more happiness in your life. That's what this book is all about.

Know Yourself
Make Sure Your Values Drive Your Decisions

". . . [Alice] was a little startled by seeing the Cheshire-Cat sitting on a bough of a tree a few yards off. . . . 'Would you tell me, please, which way I ought to go from here?' 'That depends a good deal on where you want to get to,' said the Cat. 'I don't much care where—' said Alice. 'Then it doesn't matter which way you go,' said the Cat."

LEWIS CARROLL, *Alice's Adventures in Wonderland*

Of all the costly errors you can make investing, misconceptions about yourself may be the most expensive. How well do you understand your own investing psychology? Have you figured out ways to make it work for instead of against you?

Most people don't even bother to examine how they make decisions. They don't really know *why* they're investing, much less *how* they ought to do it. Neither do they understand the importance of the investment selection process, nor the perils of holding investments when they should be sold. Without a structured process, they're guided solely by their instincts, subjecting themselves to the thoughts or whims of the day. They fail to recognize the dangers that lie ahead.

This doesn't mean, though, that effective investing has to be a dry, emotionless pursuit. On the contrary. Instead of letting impulse make your investment decisions, you can use your higher emotions (your values) to help you create a solid plan that actually contributes to fulfilling your deepest desires in life.

Consider What's Important to You

Investors most often sabotage their finances by forgetting *why* they invest. They get caught up in the game of it all, learning the lingo, chasing every hot tip, reading all the financial papers, and staring endlessly at the computer screen while trying to divine the secrets of Wall Street. But does this actually achieve their original objective? Did they ever even define an objective beyond their vague desire to have "more"?

Have you defined your own objectives? Chances are you haven't. Perhaps you've set goals, such as putting the kids through college or retiring in a few years, but if you're like most investors, you're just shooting from the hip. So let's take a step back for a moment and consider a key question: *What's important about money to you?*

The answer may seem obvious, because everyone needs money to survive. But beyond merely surviving, why do you (or did you) go to work every day? What are you trying to achieve now? What do you value that money can help you obtain? **Get clear on all this first— and then you can invest your money in ways that will help you get more of what's important to *you*.**

"The indispensable first step to getting the things you want out of life is this: Decide what you want."
BEN STEIN, Entertainer

Know Why You're Investing Before You Invest

Understanding why money is important to you—what your ultimate objectives are in attempting to multiply your wealth by investing—provides you instant riches regardless of your net worth. It gives you the self-awareness you need to make the wisest choices for

KNOW YOURSELF • *Make Sure Your Values Drive Your Decisions*

you and your family, as well as the insight you need to enjoy the money when it comes.

Without this understanding, investing can feel empty or become a nerve-wracking and all-consuming game. One man I know, whom we'll call Ed, is keenly intelligent, extremely successful, and well loved by his family. His only mistake was being born dirt poor and never outgrowing his poverty. Even though his net worth now exceeds $10 million, he still worries constantly about not having money.

Does Ed have such a high standard of living that $10 million can't meet it? No, his assets generate plenty of income to cover his expenses. Does he need tutoring in the finer points of personal finance or a remedial course in math? No, it's not that. I've shown Ed that he has nothing to worry about. He's seen in black and white how he'll never run out of money. But even though it's irrational, Ed is so fixated on having "more" that he's unwilling or unable to see his money in terms of what it can do—and is already doing—for him.

He can't get perspective on the cost of this fixation, either, and the price has been high. The anxiety has cost him his health. It's taken all the joy he could feel out of his life. He owns beautiful homes in Los Angeles and abroad, yet all he does when he goes to these lovely places is sit and watch his investment screens.

To make matters worse, Ed often takes great risks with his investments because he thinks he desperately needs more money and is willing to take huge chances to get it. Sadly, these high-risk deals usually cost him lots of money in addition to his peace of mind and health.

If I could convince Ed to see his money and himself in a new light, I would. I've tried many times to help this gentleman assess whether his worrying and obsessing help him achieve what's really important to him, but he doesn't seem to hear me. He's stuck in the past. In my opinion, this man is a tragic example of how miserable your life can be when you don't focus on what's most important to you today.

Maybe you know someone like Ed. Maybe you are someone like Ed. My point is that whether you have a modest net worth or are already rolling in clover, the financial game can really beat you up unless you're willing to seriously look at why you're playing it.

So I'll ask you again: *What's important about money to you?*

"The problem is never how to get new, innovative thoughts into your mind, but how to get old ones out."
DEE HOCK, Founder of Visa

Find Your Own Answer

If you're like most people I meet, you'll probably say money is important because it provides *safety* or *security*. It helps you buy food, shelter, and health services. Money provides the necessary ingredients to help you and your family meet your basic survival needs. No-brainers so far, right?

You might also tell me that money is important to you because it gives you *flexibility* or *freedom*. Generally, more money presents more options and choices. For example, the person supporting himself by working for minimum wage at Flippy Burger lives paycheck to paycheck. This person has few choices, little flexibility. If he wants to have a roof over his head and food in the fridge, he needs to go to work every day. Can he afford *not* to work? No. On the other hand, having money can mean you can afford to work less—or not work at all. The person with an investment nest egg may have enough income from investments to cover living expenses. This

KNOW YOURSELF • *Make Sure Your Values Drive Your Decisions*

person has flexibility and may be able to decide whether or not to work. She has many choices: she can help family members, support charity, go on extended vacations, and so on.

Money might also be important to you because it gives you *peace of mind*. You want enough money so you don't have to worry and can pour your energy into your family, friendships, profession, spiritual life, volunteer work, a hobby, or any other passion in your life. Of course, if you don't consciously understand that one of your objectives is peace of mind, then it's possible that even if you have a significant amount of money, you could sit at home worrying about your investments all day, like Ed. Clearly, in his case, money created more stress, not less—less contentment, not more. If Ed valued peace of mind over this unrelenting quest for "more," I suspect he would learn to walk away from the computer screen and go play with his grandkids or enjoy his vacation. Perhaps having "more" in some other area would enrich his life in a way that his investments never will.

Your answers to the question of why money is important to you reveal your *values*, which would be helpful to me in understanding you. In fact, any financial professional worth taking advice from will insist on knowing your values before giving any guidance. Your answers to this single key question should drive not only how you behave about your investments (will you be a screen-watcher like Ed?) but also the strategy and vehicles you employ in your investment plan.

Your answers may be different from the ones I've listed, or you may use different words to describe what you seek. On the next page is a list of values associated with money. Checkmark all the ones that seem right for you, or make up your own.

What's Important About Money to You?

____ Accomplishment
____ Achievement
____ Balance
____ Beauty
____ Choice
____ Contribution to _____
____ Flexibility
____ Freedom
____ Fulfillment
____ Leave my mark
____ Peace of mind
____ Providing for my family
____ Pursuit of knowledge
____ Safety
____ Security
____ Self-actualization
____ Self-worth
____ Time for _____

____ _____
____ _____
____ _____
____ _____

Understand *How* You Invest

As your financial adviser (at least while you're reading this book), once I know what's important about money to you, my next question is, how do you invest? In other words, what are you doing right now to achieve those objectives? If you tell me you hope to achieve safety, freedom, and peace of mind with your investments, and then you tell me you contribute the maximum amount to your 401(k) at work, you save another $500 every month, and you keep track of your monthly spending habits, your answer makes sense. Your objectives and your actions align.

However, if you then tell me that you also invest in futures contracts, short the market, trade options daily, loan money to friends and relatives, and lose money along the way (like most people who engage in these activities), your answer doesn't make sense. How do these activities contribute to your ultimate goals and values? These activities create lots of stress for investors. They make it more difficult for you to do what you really want to do. They are contrary to the values of safety, freedom, and peace of mind.

What about you? Do your investment techniques help you achieve your goals and values? They probably don't, or you wouldn't be reading this book.

Begin by asking yourself *why* you invest before you put in a dime. Otherwise, it's like driving a car without any idea of where you want to go. Then, when you're ready to choose *how* to invest, you must align those choices with your answer to the first question. Not only do most investors ignore this basic tenet of personal finance, but they also have no understanding of the real rules of investing and what steps they need to take to gain control over their investments.

By reading this book, you will no longer be like most investors.

You'll be given a proven strategy that follows the rules of investing, and you'll also be clear on what's important about money to you so you can ensure your investments and lifestyle are consistent with those values.

Invest Your Money So You Don't Outlive It

In addition to understanding why and how you are to invest, it's also critical that you know how much money you need to live—and for how long—to make sound decisions. **That means you have to track your spending, and you need to have some idea as to how long you and your spouse are going to live.**

Don't let natural reluctance to confront the big D get in the way of asking this question. It's normal to have some emotional reaction to the issue of how long you or someone you love might live, but it's important to be both practical and detached about your expected longevity if you hope to make sound financial decisions. Thinking they have some insight into their own longevity, some people tell me their family has a history of dying young, so they don't expect to be here long. Others say they don't want to live past age 80. That can turn into an interesting discussion, which helps me understand my clients better, but the truth is, nobody knows or can control how long they're going to live, regardless of heredity or fears about getting old. What we do know is that people are living longer today.

How long will you live?

If I knew the answer to that question, you'd have paid a lot more for this book. However, the following exhibit is a longevity chart issued by the IRS, and since the IRS is keenly interested in knowing how long you're going to be around to pay taxes, let's assume they know what they're talking about. (If you'd like to see the complete longevity table, please visit my Web site at www.NealFrankle.com.)

KNOW YOURSELF • *Make Sure Your Values Drive Your Decisions*

The Joint and Last Survivor Table

AGES	60	61	62	63	64	65	66	67	68	69
60	30.9	30.4	30.0	29.6	29.2	28.8	28.5	28.2	27.9	27.6
61	30.4	29.9	29.5	29.0	28.6	28.3	27.9	27.6	27.3	27.0
62	30.0	29.5	29.0	28.5	28.1	27.7	27.3	27.0	26.7	26.4
63	29.6	29.0	28.5	28.1	27.6	27.2	26.8	26.4	26.1	25.7
64	29.2	28.6	28.1	27.6	27.1	26.7	26.3	25.9	25.5	25.2
→ 65	28.8	28.3	27.7	27.2	26.7	26.2	25.8	25.4	(25.0)	24.6
66	28.5	27.9	27.3	26.8	26.3	25.8	25.3	24.9	24.5	24.1
67	28.2	27.6	27.0	26.4	25.9	25.4	24.9	24.4	24.0	23.6
68	27.9	27.3	26.7	26.1	25.5	25.0	24.5	24.0	23.5	23.1
69	27.6	27.0	26.4	25.7	25.2	24.6	24.1	23.6	23.1	22.6
70	27.4	26.7	26.1	25.4	24.8	24.3	23.7	23.2	22.7	22.2
71	27.2	26.5	25.8	25.2	24.5	23.9	23.4	22.8	22.3	21.8
72	27.0	26.3	25.6	24.9	24.3	23.7	23.1	22.5	22.0	21.4
73	26.8	26.1	25.4	24.7	24.0	23.4	22.8	22.2	21.6	21.1
74	26.6	25.9	25.2	24.5	23.8	23.1	22.5	21.9	21.3	20.8
75	26.5	25.7	25.0	24.3	23.6	22.9	22.3	21.6	21.0	20.5
76	26.3	25.6	24.8	24.1	23.4	22.7	22.0	21.4	20.8	20.2
77	26.2	25.4	24.7	23.9	23.2	22.5	21.8	21.2	20.6	19.9
78	26.1	25.3	24.6	23.8	23.1	22.4	21.7	21.0	20.3	19.7
79	26.0	25.2	24.4	23.7	22.9	22.2	21.5	20.8	20.1	19.5
80	25.9	25.1	24.3	23.6	22.8	22.1	21.3	20.6	20.0	19.3
81	25.8	25.0	24.2	23.4	22.7	21.9	21.2	20.5	19.8	19.1
82	25.8	24.9	24.1	23.4	22.6	21.8	21.1	20.4	19.7	19.0
83	25.7	24.9	24.1	23.3	22.5	21.7	21.0	20.2	19.5	18.8
84	25.6	24.8	24.0	23.2	22.4	21.6	20.9	20.1	19.4	18.7
85	25.6	24.8	23.9	23.1	22.3	21.6	20.8	20.1	19.3	18.6

Source: *The Federal Register*, Department of Treasury, Internal Revenue Service, 26 CFR parts 1, 54 and 602, Required Distributions from Retirement Plans; Final Rule 4/17/02

You'll notice that I've marked the chart with a couple of arrows and a circle. It shows the hypothetical example of a couple aged 65 and 68. In such a case, at least one of the two people can expect to live another 25 years.[1] (Now, if you're 68 years old and your spouse is 27, you may not find your longevity expectancy on this table, but I wouldn't worry about it. Just enjoy yourself!)

I have good news and bad news about this longevity table. The good and bad news are one and the same. As I hinted earlier, the numbers presented in the table are probably too conservative. People live longer and longer. Medical science has done an excellent job of expanding our life span. In fact, since 1900, advances in health science have extended the average life span by 31 years.[2] That's just amazing, if you ask me.

Now consider this next chart:

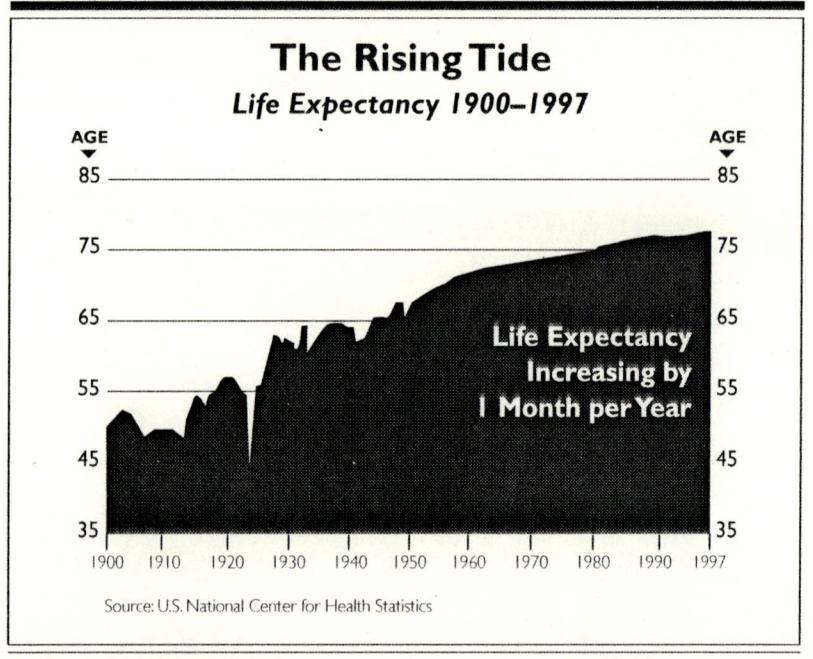

---

[1] Taken from IRS Publication 590.
[2] Life-span data from 1995 U.S. Census "Statistical Bulletin," averaging all U.S. races provided.

This chart shows what's been happening to the average life span since 1900. A person born in 1900 could expect to live to the ripe old age of 47. A person born in 1985 can expect to live to the age of 75. We eat better, exercise more, and have better medical care.

The point is, you should plan on living many years. **Plan to live longer than the numbers in the IRS table indicate.** Why? Because if you plan to be around for 30 years, and you get hit by a bus next week, you have no more financial worries. If you plan on living 30 more years and you do live 30 more years, you also have no problem. But if you plan on living 30 more years and live 38 more instead, you've got a problem. You have to plan so you don't outlive your income and assets.

Now that you have a realistic picture of how long you'll need your money to last, you'll better understand which investments are most appropriate for your needs.

Once You Know What's Important to You

If money is important to you because it helps provide freedom, security, flexibility, less stress, and other similar values, then you're in the right place. This book will help you achieve that.

If, however, your "values" include making a fast buck or something else along those lines, I suggest you go ahead and get your cash quickly by promptly returning this book for a refund. What you'll learn here may earn you more money than you're earning now, and it may help you do so more quickly, but it probably won't satisfy the quick-buck types. I really can't help those people, so if you're one of them, I wish you good luck, and may the force be with you. (Bye, now.)

If you've come to this book for the right reasons, we're truly on the same page. Now that you understand how your most important emotions and desires should influence your investment strategy (and we'll get into more detail on the actual strategy later), the next chapter will take an in-depth look at how to keep our more petty emotions out of the equation.

Points of Interest

- Before you hit the road, decide where you want to go. Know what's important about money to you before you invest.
- Once you know what's important about money to you, make sure your investments work to support your values—not to counteract them.
- If money is important to you because you value safety, freedom, less stress, and flexibility, it would make no sense for you to invest for the quick buck, invest based on hot tips, or ignore your investments. None of these techniques will help you be happy. You need an alternate technique.

Exercises

1. Ask yourself what's important about money to you. Write down at least three answers. Use the list on page 16 to help, if need be.
2. Ask your spouse the same question and record his or her responses—three at the least.
3. List five of your largest investments (excluding your residence), and write about how owning these investments helps you achieve what's most important about money to you.
4. Track your monthly budget. (If you don't already have a system for this, set one up immediately to record your expenses.)
5. Determine your spouse's and your own expected longevity.

Face Facts
Base Your Decisions on How the Market Really Works

"If you can't accept losing, you can't win."
VINCE LOMBARDI, Football Coach

No doubt you're reading this book so you can invest more wisely and ultimately make more money. That's a given. But let's also agree that if you invest in anything other than bank CDs, you'll lose money sooner or later. This is also a fact of life, one that comes under the heading of *Things We'd Rather Not Be True*. Yet it's going to happen, no matter how brilliant your mother says you are. Investing for significant reward always entails some risk.

Most investors know this, though the majority is unwilling to acknowledge it. Because they can't accept this reality of investing, it lurks below the surface like some kind of financial bogeyman. This opens the door to fear running the show: fear of losing money, fear of making the wrong choice, fear of missing out.

But if you can simply face the fact that at times *you will lose money*, you can focus on the single most important factor for minimizing those losses when they occur—to sell before what could have been a small loss becomes a huge one.[1]

Some people have a system they follow for choosing investments, but few have any selling discipline, and those who do often throw their rules away exactly when they need them most. This is like going on an ocean cruise without taking life rafts—or cutting the rafts loose just as a storm approaches. Do this enough times, and eventually you'll get wet or worse. Guaranteed.

---

[1] Hersh Shefrin, *Beyond Greed and Fear* (New York: Oxford University Press, 2002).

Most people are running around chasing the latest hot tip and trying to figure out what to *buy*. Yet finding the "right" investment is not the answer to minimizing inevitable losses, because you usually don't lose the big money by buying the wrong investment. Let's face it: *You record the biggest losses when you don't sell when you should.*

This is why buy-and-hold strategies are bogus. Yeah, I said it: Buying and holding is a bunch of baloney because it doesn't encourage you to sell when you should. The strategy works only when the market is doing well—if stocks continue to climb in value. But if you buy then hold because you don't monitor performance at all, that's dumb. And if you buy then hold *despite* poor performance, that's, well, dumber. There's simply no guarantee that any investment will perform so well that it never needs to be reviewed again. But buying and holding is attractive to many people because it allows them to put their heads in the sand and feel good about it—for a while, at least.

"Facts do not cease to exist because they are ignored."
ALDOUS HUXLEY, Novelist and Critic

Why are most of us so fond of doing nothing? It's just a quirk of human nature. Researchers have found, as you'd expect, that investors feel bad when they lose money. But all things being equal, meaning if the loss is the same, they feel better about a loss if they lose the money because they didn't act than if they lose money because of something they've done.[2] In other words, an investor will feel better if she holds (does nothing) and loses money than if she sells (does something) and loses money.

Assume Mary buys an investment for $100,000 and later sells, realizing a loss of $10,000. She feels worse than if she'd held a

---

[2] Hersh Shefrin, *Beyond Greed and Fear.*

FACE FACTS • *Base Your Decisions on How the Market Really Works*

$100,000 investment that declined in value by $10,000 (and stayed down). This is nonsense, isn't it? It's not as if there's any tangible difference between the two: the money's gone regardless. And if you think about it, she's just as responsible in either case: Doing nothing—such as deciding to hold—is just as causative as taking some action. (Of course, some people do nothing because they don't know what to do. This book will help with that problem, too.)

Let's be clear that in this example, the hold ultimately yielded the same loss—not "just a paper loss." That's another issue altogether, but no less serious. Referring to paper losses just means you're waiting to see if the market will change and you won't have to recognize the loss that exists today. It's not real until you cash out, you think. Have you ever deluded yourself like this?

Investors often hold onto their losses to avoid pain, but this avoidance is what amplifies the pain. Have you ever held onto a stock "until it gets back to what I paid for it," only to see the price topple further? The lesson? **Don't let this irrational preference for inaction immobilize you, make you complacent, or otherwise keep you from selling when you ought to minimize your losses. Adopt a method for getting into** *and out of* **the market—and then stick to it.**

Even experts and professionals fall victim to this character defect. I've mentioned the CAN SLIM method for investing in stocks. It's a widely respected method, and investors who follow CAN SLIM are instructed to sell any stock that declines in price by 8 percent or more below the stock's purchase price. This is O'Neil's cardinal rule, meant to protect capital.[3]

Many people who subscribe to this strategy are well-read. Typically, they study O'Neil's books and read his daily newspaper, the *Investor's Business Daily*. Some attend his lectures frequently. Do you think most of the investors who profess to follow the CAN SLIM method actually follow that capital protection rule?

[3] William J. O'Neil, *How to Make Money in Stocks*, 1st ed. (New York: McGraw-Hill, 1991).

I don't think they do. Even the educated and supposedly stock-savvy still fall prey to their fear.

How do I know? Because I've joined many newsgroups to discuss CAN SLIM over the years. Par for the course, the participants in such groups say they've studied the system and claim to use it to manage their own money. But many of these "experts" abandon the founder's cardinal sell rule, which amazes me. I even read a newsgroup partner's post about holding a stock and sitting on a 30 percent loss. It made me want to scream! Investors who are true to the methodology and use the CAN SLIM method should never have any loss much greater than 8 percent.

Isn't it ridiculous to use only part of a proven method and expect good results? Can you imagine a doctor taking out your tonsils and performing only his favorite part of the operation? How about an airline pilot using only the part she liked best about the landing procedures? Or the post office employee only delivering your mail, not picking it up as well? **When you choose your system,** *use it.*

"If you want to know what a man is really like, take notice how he acts when he loses money."
W. C. FIELDS, Comedian

Stay Off the Emotional Roller Coaster

Adopting an investment methodology and then using only parts of it usually has its roots in fear, just as most poor investment behavior does. Have you been letting your baser instincts rule your investment choices until now? Consider the exhibit on the next page. Do you recognize this train of thought?

FACE FACTS • Base Your Decisions on How the Market Really Works

Happy Trading . . .

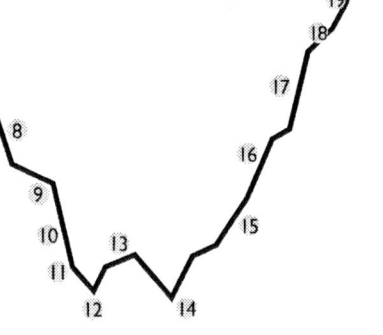

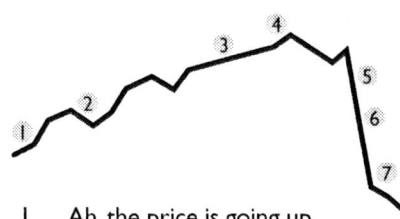

1. Ah, the price is going up, let's watch the market.

2. The trend is holding— I'll buy at the next consolidation.

3. Damn! I missed the consolidation, but if I wait any longer, I won't profit from the trend. LET'S BUY!

4. Good thing I didn't wait!

5. I'll use this correction to increase my position . . .

6. Brilliant! At this price, let's double!

7. Ouch. As soon as it goes back up, I'm selling out!

8. I don't believe it! It's down to 8-$^1/_4$! It's hit its absolute bottom!

9. OK. Let's wait for it to recover— otherwise this will have to be a really looooooooong-term investment.

10. What is the SEC doing about this?!?!?!?!

11. Enough! I'm selling out and staying out.

12. Good thing I sold everything!

13. It's going to tank again anyway.

14. Told you so.

15. You what???

16. What the hell???

17. More crazies who are going to get taken to the cleaners.

18. This is it! I knew this was going to happen all along!

19. Drat! I'll buy in again. It's cheaper than last time anyhow.

If this looks all too familiar to you, you've probably been making most of your investment decisions based on your immediate emotions (or your broker's emotions)—and you're like the majority of other investors.[4] Can you see how this leads to greater losses?

Does this mean you should just ignore the market and follow some rigid plan: full steam ahead and damn the torpedoes? Of course not. **It's important to consider market conditions as you invest and divest, whether it's in stocks or mutual funds.** Reacting emotionally to events is hugely different from following an investment method that's sensitive to what's happening in the real world.

When you have an investment method, you know that everything you buy eventually will be sold. The only question is when. When you make a decision to sell, it's based on the best information available at the time. You have to accept that after you sell, new information may become available that might have led you to reach a different decision—but you must take action anyway.

Don't Ignore the Market

As it is commonly practiced, the strategy of buy and hold, or what I like to call "buy and forget it," amounts to ignoring the market—and your mounting losses. "Here, buy this, and it's such a good investment that now all you have to do is hold," many professionals say, encouraging you just to grin and file your statements when they come in the mail, regardless of the percentage gained or lost.

---

[4] On the other hand, if you don't see yourself as someone who makes investment decisions emotionally, you may be falling into the trap of long-term buy and hold (which is really just a nice way of saying *buy and forget about it,* as detailed in this chapter) or asset allocation (which is a useful concept but rarely plays out as planned in real life). As you'll see, people who rely on these investment methods are in almost as much danger as the folks investing purely on emotion.

When the market broadly advances, buy and forget it works. But the market doesn't always advance. When the market turns, most investors and brokers are caught with their pants down. They don't have any alternative strategy, so they cling to the buy-and-forget-it fairy tale.

> *"Even if you're on the right track, you'll get run over if you just sit there."*
> WILL ROGERS, Humorist

At first, advisers rationalize buy-and-forget-it strategies to clients even in a declining market. If anything, many advisers tell their clients to "use the market decline as an opportunity to buy more shares and take advantage of the great prices."

This reminds me of the children's story of the three little pigs and the wolf. If you buy and forget it, you simply believe that the big bad wolf (a huge market drop) won't ever come calling. This is wishful thinking. Remember what many people did in March 2000? They simply held their investments and watched as their net worth vanished.

On average, a bear (or should I say wolf?) market visits investors 4 out of every 10 years.[5] Do you think what happened in the market between 2000 and 2002 was an anomaly? From 1961 through 1990, the market had eight major declines averaging more than 30 percent. And over a longer period of time, from 1899 to 1990 as illustrated in the chart on the next page, you see a total of 23 declines, all greater than 20 percent, over 99 years.

---

[5] Michael B. O'Higgins and John McCarty, *Beating the Dow with Bonds* (New York: HarperBusiness, 1999), xiii.

Market Declines 1899–1990

High Price	High Date	Low Price	Low Date	% Decline
2999.75	7/16/90	2365.10	10/11/90	−21.2%
2722.42	8/25/87	1738.74	10/19/87	−36.1%
1024.05	4/27/81	776.92	8/12/82	−24.1%
1014.79	9/21/76	742.12	2/28/78	−26.1%
1051.70	1/11/73	577.60	12/6/74	−45.1%
985.21	12/3/68	631.16	5/26/70	−35.9%
995.15	2/9/66	744.32	10/7/66	−25.2%
726.01	1/3/62	535.76	6/26/62	−26.2%
212.50	5/29/46	163.12	10/9/46	−23.2%
133.59	1/10/41	106.34	12/23/41	−20.4%
152.80	1/3/40	111.84	6/10/40	−26.8%
158.41	11/12/38	121.44	4/8/39	−23.3%
194.40	3/10/37	113.64	2/24/37	−41.5%
110.74	2/5/34	85.51	7/26/34	−22.8%
381.17	9/3/29	41.22	7/8/32	−89.2%
119.62	11/3/19	63.90	8/24/21	−46.6%
110.15	11/21/16	65.95	12/19/17	−40.1%
83.43	3/20/14	54.22	2/24/15	−35.0%
94.15	9/30/12	72.11	6/11/13	−23.4%
100.53	2/19/09	72.94	9/25/11	−27.4%
103.00	11/19/06	53.00	11/15/07	−48.5%
78.26	6/17/01	42.15	11/9/03	−46.1%
77.61	9/7/1899	52.96	9/24/1900	−31.8%

Number of Down Years 1899–1998: 35
Number of Up Years 1899–1998: 63

Source: Michael B. O'Higgins, *Beating the Dow with Bonds* (New York: HarperBusiness, 1999), pg. 80.

Most people, including financial advisers, don't have any kind of model for interpreting the market or understanding what's happening because they're taught to ignore the market. The

FACE FACTS • Base Your Decisions on How the Market Really Works

professionals base their recommendations solely on the past and hope that history repeats itself. Hope springs eternal. Too bad money doesn't.

Let's look at the period from March 2000 through September 2002, which offers a lifelong lesson in how buying and holding can really be fatal to your financial dreams.

To be fair, in the market prior to the year 2000, people made a lot of money buying and holding tech stocks. During that time, there were many 20 percent corrections—periods when the market declined by up to 20 percent—and the market did come back. As a result, those people who held onto their stocks made money.

But the people who held on did so with total abandon. They didn't hold for any reason other than they believed in the buy-and-forget-it strategy. They were holding when the "wolf" was on vacation. Bull markets help many people confuse luck with intelligence. They had no basis to hold their stocks or funds. They had no awareness of what was going on in the market, and worse yet, they didn't think it mattered!

Gradually, the market began to fall apart. Like all bubbles, the market popped. Eventually, any company that didn't post high enough profits (and heaven forbid they post losses) got hammered. Their stock cratered.

At first, many investors held and kept holding as their net worth imploded. Some people even invested more money as their shares declined in value. Even many Wall Street analysts in message boards across the country urged people to load up on stocks or at least hold onto their stocks as the market posted triple-digit declines on a daily basis.

Those people who heeded the words of such "market gurus" saw their wealth shrivel and their losses grow. The few who got out when the market told them to had peace of mind and profited handsomely.

But the market meltdown that began in March 2000 wasn't the first time something like this happened—and it won't be the last. Just one example: An elite group of stocks that did very well in the 1960s, dubbed the "Nifty Fifty," didn't fare so well during the 1973-1974 recession, declining by 71 to 90 percent. Did these stocks come back? One of the Nifty Fifty stocks was Eastman Kodak. From 1962 to 1973, the stock went from $18 to $121, but during the 1973-1974 bear market, it was mauled. The stock took nine and a half years to reverse the downtrend and another four years before it even got close to its 1973 high. That's a 13-year wait. Can you put your retirement on hold for 13 years?

Polaroid is another example. From July 1962 to its peak in November 1969, the stock soared 1,190 percent! But the stock was pulverized in the 1973-1974 bear market. It dropped 90 percent in only 15 months. In the next 26 years, the stock never hit a new high. On October 12, 2001, Polaroid filed for Chapter 11 bankruptcy.[6]

Do you think things will be different tomorrow? Do you have any reason to expect the high-flyers from the tech bubble to come back to reclaim their past glory? Of past winners, less than half ever reach a new high after a correction—and when they have, it's taken five years or more on average. Of these, less than 14 percent have gone on to lead the market again.[7]

In short, if you buy and forget a fallen angel, the odds are squarely against you that the stock will be a leader again in the future. If the only reason you own a stock is because it has fallen in price and you "know" it will come back, beware. That's not a reason based in the realities of the market.

---

[6] T. M. F. Runkle, "The Not So Nifty Fifty or Leisure Suits, Disco, and Bear Markets," *The Motley Fool* (June 27, 1997), http://www.fool.com/FRIBBLE/1997/FRIBBLE970627.htm.

[7] William J. O'Neil, *How to Make Money in Stocks*.

Company Man

When investors own shares of the companies they work for, they can be especially gullible about the buy-and-hold myth. Some stick by their employer's stock with an almost cultish conviction. (WorldCom, Sun, AOL, Cisco, and Intel come to mind.) Some of these might be great companies, but if an investor's goals are to have freedom and joy without having to worry about money, does it make sense to have every egg in that one basket?

Let me illustrate. Jim, a client of mine, needs $200,000 to live well each year. Jim's net worth exceeds $10 million because of stock options he received while working. Jim can sell the options and invest the $10 million at 5 percent (for this example, we'll ignore taxes). If he does so, he'll earn $200,000 every year.

Congratulations, Jim, you're done!

In other words, all Jim has to do to retire right now is to cash out. If he does, he'll also reduce risk. If, on the other hand, he holds onto the stock, he runs the risk of seeing his $10 million turn into $2 million or less. If that happened, his dreams would be finished. He wouldn't be able to retire.

It's also in the realm of possibility that if Jim holds the stock, the $10 million could turn into $20 million. But this potential upside won't change his life. Oh, sure, it would be great to have an extra $10 million. But the first $10 million achieves his goals of freedom and joy. Why risk those things, which he values most? It doesn't seem worth it to me.

Instead of buying and holding, for whatever reason— company loyalty, a preference for doing nothing, fear of making the wrong choices—find yourself a method you can count on, and then hold onto *that.* Place your allegiance in something that has a better chance of helping you achieve your dreams.

How to Find a Strategy That Works

I've reviewed all the newsletters with no-gimmick investment advice. If buy and forget it was the way to go, I'd expect to see one espousing that idea to be number one in performance. I found the exact opposite to be true. Granted, among the newsletters that advise investors on mutual fund investing, only one was consistent in helping its readers achieve excellent returns over many years—and that one certainly didn't suggest that investors buy and forget it.

I'm referring to the *NoLoad Fund*X* newsletter (www.fundx.com). This letter's performance was excellent. In fact, on a risk-adjusted basis, this publication was ranked second out of 98 over 5 years, first of 67 over 10 years, second of 42 over 15 years, and first of 17 over 20 years.[8] Clearly, this newsletter has something of value to offer.

How do the folks at *NoLoad Fund*X* pump out such outstanding results, and how can you benefit from their method?

They use an upgrading system, wherein you buy funds while they have very strong short-term results (*NoLoad Fund*X* computes a blended one-year, nine-month, six-month, three-month, and one-month return).

One strategy the newsletter suggests you use is to invest in five of the strongest funds within one class (conservative, moderate, or aggressive) and continue to hold onto those funds as long as they outperform other funds in their class. When the funds that are held start underperforming, the newsletter instructs you to sell and move into the most current winners. That's the short view of how this works.

The *Hulbert Financial Digest*, which has tracked investment

---

[8] Mark Hulbert, *Hulbert Financial Digest*, September 2003, cited in http://www.fundx.com/hulb.cfm.

[9] Timothy Middleton, *Mutual Fund, MSN Money* posted on http://www.moneycentral.msn.com/content/p28782.asp?Printer.

newsletter recommendations for decades, said that since 1989, *NoLoad Fund*X* newsletter delivered the best risk-adjusted returns of any investment newsletter, and the second best returns overall.[9]

What explains their stellar performance? They don't buy and forget it!

The organization that runs *NoLoad Fund*X* is the DAL Investment Company. They've done research over more than 32 years and observed that few fund managers consistently excel. Instead, they found that only a small number of professional money managers ever invested in the right sectors of the market at the right time. In an extensive report, the Funds Management Research Centre came to the same conclusion.[10] Why is that?

Because each manager has a style that may work sometimes, but won't work in all market environments. That's why mutual fund leadership shifts. Also, economic conditions change over time, and most fund managers don't change their style in accordance with what's happening in the market. They stick to their own vision.

In contrast, the *NoLoad Fund*X* strategy incrementally moves into those mutual funds that are outperforming and out of those that are underperforming.

These folks decided to simply listen to the market. The market shifts. You can either buy and forget it and ignore this reality (for results of this, consult your investment statements!) or become sensitive to those changes and take appropriate action.[11]

---

[10] David Allen, Tim Brailsford, Ron Bird, and Robert Faff, "A Review of the Research on the Past Performance of Managed Funds," Funds Management Research Centre of the Securities Industry Research Centre of the Asia Pacific, September 2002 (revised June 2003).

[11] While I think the *NoLoad Fund*X* newsletter is an excellent tool, I do not rely on its methodology completely. The newsletter recommends people stay invested in the top funds 100 percent of the time—even if the market is in decline and those funds are losing money. I believe that investors are better served by taking the market's temperature and only investing in the top funds when the market demonstrates strength.

Don't Try to Outsmart the Market

I've seen countless examples of people ruining their finances by not responding responsibly to the market—they're like children throwing tantrums instead of adults with the skills to acknowledge their emotions yet make decisions based on more than their immediate excitement or disappointment.

There are two critical mistakes to avoid: *ignoring* the market or *thinking you know better* than the market.

The second problem, believing you can somehow outthink the market, is plain folly. I'm reminded of Mark, a man I met at a seminar in late 1998. Mark loved Disney. I mean, Mark *loved* Disney. He was crazy about their theme parks, merchandising, and films, so he bought a *lot* of their stock. Disney, he argued, is a unique company with unlimited growth potential. The market didn't agree, and the stock weakened. From over $40 per share, the stock sank to below $30. I asked Mark to consider what the market was saying about Disney stock, and he told me the market was wrong. As those words left his mouth, I could almost hear the market whisper in a menacing way, "You talkin' to *me?*"

Sure enough, the stock continued to sink and its share price dropped below $15. But three years later and sporting a 50 percent loss, Mark still tells everyone who'll listen how wonderful Disney is and how ignorant the market really is. Mark may be right, but he's lost a great deal of money to show for it. Mark just can't swallow being wrong and he pays a high price for his pride.

Don't Try to Be Perfect, Either

Remember Ed? He once bought stock in a company that makes computer chips. Now, Ed is a smart man. He read about the company, knew something about the industry, and determined that this company was the way to go.

FACE FACTS • Base Your Decisions on How the Market Really Works

He bought the stock at $9 a share. Eighteen months later, the stock was trading at $75 a share. Ed was now sitting on a $200,000 profit.

I suggested that Ed put in a stop-loss order to sell the stock if it dropped below $65 per share—this would protect his profits. The market was iffy at the time, and the stock wasn't acting that healthy. On top of that, other firms had announced their immediate plans to compete with Ed's company. And to put the cork in the bottle, the SEC announced it was going to audit the firm for some irregularities.

Ed, a smart but greedy man, still had high hopes for this company, and his hopes could have been well founded. But I made my suggestions based on what I knew about the market, the company, and Ed. I knew that the most important thing about money to him was security. Ed was blinded by greed and lost sight of his values.

Had Ed placed the stop-loss order for $65, the stock would have automatically been sold for him once the price hit $65 or less. He insisted that the company was poised for greatness, and he refused to place the stop-loss.

The stock hit $64, but did Ed sell? No. He told me he would get out if the stock ever climbed back up to $75. You can guess why: He didn't want to be wrong.

When the stock hit $60, his wife insisted he place the stop-loss order at $55. The stock was sold at $55, and Ed made a tidy profit of over $170,000.

I consider this a victory for Ed. Did Ed sell at the best time? No. He sold a little late. But nobody sells at the ultimate best time. And it could have been much worse for Ed. Within four weeks, the stock was trading at less than $10 per share. Of course, he was disappointed that he'd sold at $55 rather than $75. But he should have been thrilled that he sold at $55 rather than $10! Had the stock gone up instead and reached $75 or $80 after he sold at $55, he would have been miserable, too, and probably would have had a few choice words for me and his wife.

You can see that shooting for perfection is a surefire guarantee for disappointment. Because of Ed's illusion that he could find the exact best time to sell, he was doomed to be miserable no matter what. He simply had to decide to be miserable and safe (and wealthy in this case) by listening to what the market was saying, or be miserable and broke by ignoring what the market had to say in the matter.

Are you willing to be less than perfect? If you are willing to accept your mistakes, you're well on your way to being a good investor.

You must accept the fact that you'll never sell at the exact perfect time. Be content with that. Easy to say, hard to do. The easiest way to implement this is to invest using a single method—and never waver.

Woulda, Coulda, Shoulda

Many investors bury their heads. Others compare alternatives incorrectly, especially in market extremes. They experience losses or foregone gains and, rather than accept what happened, allow it to infect their thinking. In a bear market, they complain that they could have done better in a CD than in the market. In a bull market, they compare their "lousy" 15 percent performance to the high-tech fund that doubled.

This thinking will absolutely lead to disappointment and inappropriate decisions, like two ship owners comparing their vessels. One owns a speedboat and the other owns an oil tanker. Should the speedboat owner complain about his ship's inability to haul two million barrels of oil? Should the tanker owner complain about not being able to travel quickly?

FACE FACTS • *Base Your Decisions on How the Market Really Works*

You can see how ridiculous such comparisons are. Yet investors do this all the time. They continue to be great Monday-morning quarterbacks and continue to lose money as a result.

Think of the driver who tries to outsmart other cars on the road by furiously changing from one lane to another. Have you ever been annoyed by someone cutting you off in traffic, then strangely satisfied when you passed the same car later, either stuck behind some slow driver or pulled over by the cops?

It happens in the grocery store, too. In one line, the delay might be with the cashier, so it seems as if that line doesn't move at all. If you move out of that line to another, chances are you'll move just in time to get behind that line's delayer. You've either experienced this yourself or seen some other knucklehead in the store trying to beat the odds.

It works the same way with investments. Regardless of the method you use, you'll never be in all the funds or stocks with the highest return at all times. Hopping from method to method won't get you a better aggregate return, and it's sure to give you more than a few headaches.

If you jettison one investment strategy after another in search of the perfect strategy (one that makes you money in all situations), you'll simply lose lots of money. Why? Because you'll jump around from one idea to the next just in time to experience each method's weakness. Just when your real estate investments drop, you move to the stock market, and when the market goes bum, you move on to something else—without a plan, willy nilly. **All investments are cyclical, so you'd do better to follow a system that capitalizes on this fact rather than changing your strategy with every dip in return.** In effect, people who switch all the time are stuck with lousy returns—just like the anxious shopper who ends up stuck in the slow line.

Reality Check...The Hard Part

Most people agree that jumping from one investment method to the next is bad medicine—and half of them actually practice what they preach.

The other half say they understand it until game time. These are the folks who are comfortable with investing until they actually lose money, or until another investment outperforms their own. Their risk comfort level changes as the market changes. These folks change investing methods faster than my brother-in-law puts gas in his tank—and he drives a Hummer. These folks want to be 100 percent invested in the hottest stocks, 100 percent of the time. This is impossible—and a surefire recipe for disaster. The better route? To have one method that accounts for changing market environments, and to stick to that method.

Yet there's a difference between staying with something that makes sense (such as a sound investment method) and foolish consistency (such as holding onto a stock that should be dumped), which Ralph Waldo Emerson told us ages ago is "the hobgoblin of little minds." In the year 2000 and for a few years after, we had an awful market. Most people would have been better off cutting their losses and just sitting it out. (And in doing so, they could have sidestepped most of the damage.) But many investors saw their portfolios sliced by 50 percent or more because they were foolishly consistent, holding onto their stock. Alternately, investors who made an effort to listen to what the market was telling them were able to avoid most of that loss.

Sometimes the market is just not attractive. If you insist on always taking action, it can cost you a great deal more than money. It's like trying to buck some force of nature.

My father was a recreational pilot. One foggy morning he went up in his small plane with two friends to do them a favor. He was instrument rated, which means he was licensed to fly in extremely

FACE FACTS • Base Your Decisions on How the Market Really Works

bad conditions. There was zero visibility that day, but he went up anyway. I remember how foggy it was because I literally couldn't see five feet in front of me as I drove to Granada Hills High School in Southern California.

I'm sure that as he took off, he thought he would land safely that day. But the chances of a catastrophe occurring go up tenfold in bad conditions. A wise pilot, willing to take no for an answer, recognizes the dangers and lives to fly another day. These are patient people. Other pilots ignore the circumstances. They may have a great deal of resolve in the face of poor odds, but they usually don't live to be old pilots. Indeed, my father's determination cost him his life that day.

With the market, no matter how smart, talented, or courageous you think you are, you're safest to have a set plan for what to do in inclement weather. Certainly, you don't go up insisting the skies are clear.

Consider these conditions: the market is very weak. What are your choices?

Option 1. Do something! Short the market. When you short the market, you "bet" that the market will decline in value. You borrow securities and sell today at the current high prices, even though you don't currently own the securities. Then, when prices are lower, you buy the securities and return them to the person you borrowed them from. In essence, you're selling high and buying low, but you're selling before you buy. It's difficult to short the market and make money. Most investors lose money when they do so.[12] Of course, it's possible for you to make money by going short, but is doing so in line with your life goals of having more safety, flexibility, and less stress? Probably not.

Option 2. Do something! Invest in bonds until the market improves. Yes, you could. But this option is also not without risk. If

---
[12] William J. O'Neil, *How to Make Money in Stocks*, 113.

rates happen to be low, you take the risk of rates going up while you hold the bonds, causing your investment to lose value. (For a thorough explanation, see appendix B, "How Bonds Work.") Perhaps your goal is to stay in bonds as long as the market is stormy, then move back to stocks as soon as the market picks up. It's possible to do this, but it, too, is risky since it's very tough to time it exactly. You could lose more than you hoped to pick up in added interest earnings.

Option 3. Do something! Lock the money up in bank deposits until the market improves. While your money is in the bank, you won't have to pay your adviser, and you'll enjoy a higher interest rate than if it was held in the money market account at your brokerage. If you know exactly when the market is going to turn around, great! But if you don't have a crystal ball, you have a problem.

If you lock the money up in a three-year CD, for example, how do you know that the market won't turn around in one year? If it does, what will you do? If you break the CD, you'll have to pay the bank a penalty. Locking up the money prevents you from being able to take advantage of the market when it demonstrates strength again.

Let me be direct. All of these alternatives are the offspring of misguided thinking and pure emotional behavior. Anyone taking these options thinks he or she knows exactly what's going to happen and for how long. The reality is, you can't know these things—nobody can.

On the other hand, a person who's willing to listen to the market should be content to, *at times, keep the money in a money market account.* It doesn't ever make sense to take undue risk with those dollars earmarked for growth. If the market is rotten, why chance it? Given your other options, sometimes the money market is the best alternative.

You have to look at yourself and be honest. If you don't have an investment plan, you'll react emotionally when you experience inevitable losses. These reactions will create greater losses. You need an alternative. I can help you achieve what's most important to you if you're willing to be honest with yourself and if you're willing to stop doing the things that are hurting you most.

Using what you'll learn in this book, you'll know what to do, what's right for you. You can have more safety, freedom, and flexibility, as well as less stress. You can reduce the risk you face in investing. You can achieve your goals. You can avoid the "big mistake." If the market is weak, I can help you avoid catastrophe. However, I can't make you piles of money in a sick stock market, and I can't show you how to beat the market year in and year out.

I think it should be painfully clear to you by now that left to your own devices, as good as your intentions are, your emotions will ruin your finances. You need an alternative. Investors forget, make light of, or ignore the extent to which their emotions affect their investment decisions—and it costs them a fortune.

If you want a way out, the first principle is honesty. **Be honest about yourself, about how you're currently making decisions, and about understanding what it really costs you.** Only then can you have an opportunity to take your investing to the next level.

Points of Interest

- Faced with the option of either doing something and being wrong or doing nothing and being wrong, most people prefer to do nothing and be wrong. This explains why it's so difficult for most people to sell.
- Most of the costliest mistakes investors can make stem from their inability to sell when appropriate. People delay selling to delay feeling the pain, and by doing so, they often sit and watch a small loss become a large one.

- Even experts can find it difficult to stick to their selling discipline.
- Investors tend to sell their winning investments quickly to realize their gain and hold onto their losing funds to avoid feeling the anguish associated with their loss.
- If you have a high percentage of your wealth in one stock, evaluate whether your action is helping you move toward reaching your goals.

Exercises

1. List three examples of when you invested based on your emotions.
2. List three examples of when you didn't sell an investment because of your emotions.
3. List the results of each of these mistakes.

Pay Attention
Listen to the Market, Not the Media

*"One accurate measurement is worth
a thousand expert opinions."*
GRACE MURRAY HOPE, Rear Admiral, U.S. Navy

The media can lead you down the path of self-destruction if you allow it. Many investors entertain the misconception that they can make better investment decisions if they read the daily newspaper, watch CNBC, and subscribe to *Money* magazine. As you'll see, the opposite is true.

Even if some of the media commentators did know what they were talking about, how would you decide who to listen to? It seems as if everyone on TV is an "expert" on the stock market, yet they all disagree with each other. Many people find that frustrating, including me. Who should you believe?

In my opinion, you don't need to believe any of them.

Some people refer to the advice given on radio, TV, and the Internet as financial pornography. I don't know if I'd go that far, but **I do agree that most financial advice I hear in the media is just noise.** Most market commentators speak without using any real method for interpreting market fluctuations. As a result, what they're reporting is really just their opinion.

Sure, they have a right to their opinions—yet many of the commentators present their opinions as facts, which becomes a problem when people act accordingly. It's simply dangerous to rely on the media to shape your investment plan.

The Dangerous Illusions

We all create illusions in our minds, and the media gets the Oscar for "Best Supporting Role." The tragedy is that most of us make the mistake of thinking those illusions are facts. Then we hold onto them and defend our position in an almost extreme manner. This makes our ability to reason and see reality much more difficult.

In the book *Inevitable Illusions: How Mistakes of Reason Rule Our Minds*, author Massimo Piattelli-Palmarini shows how our actions are affected by the way things are presented to us.[1] One case study detailed the results from two groups of doctors who were presented the same information in two different manners.

Hypothetically, a new treatment had been discovered for a serious disease, and that treatment was an operation. The doctors in Group A were told there was a 7 percent mortality rate within five years of the operation. Doctors in Group B, on the other hand, were told that there was a 93 percent survival rate within five years of the operation.

Doctors in Group A hesitated to suggest the operation, while doctors in Group B were more quick to recommend it, despite the fact that there was no difference in either the disease or the treatment. The two answers were basically the same, yet they seemed different because of what's called *framing*—not the content of the information, but the context.

Keep this in mind as you look at financial coverage in the press. Stories are framed in an exciting way to seduce you into buying a publication or tuning in to a show. Most of the financial media is no different from the sensational rags you see in supermarket checkout stands. They just want to sell newspapers and airtime—they don't care what they have to print in order to do so, and they probably don't give a lot of thought to the impact of their

---

[1] Massimo Piattelli-Palmarini, *Inevitable Illusions: How Mistakes of Reason Rule Our Minds* (New York: John Wiley & Sons, 1994).

stories' framing. They get away with this because they have little accountability.

Financial professionals who provide investment advice to the public are held accountable for what they say by various government agencies. But media of general circulation is exempt.[2] In other words, they can print or say whatever they want without any responsibility whatsoever—it's "just" an opinion. That's nice to know, isn't it?

Is the media helpful in understanding the general health of the market? What do you think?

On September 1, 1998, the morning edition of the *San Francisco Chronicle* headlined "Panic Hammers Market," reporting on the prior day. What impression do you get when you see that headline? You probably think we're headed for the second depression!

But the evening edition of the same paper proclaimed in its headline, "Stocks Bounce Back: Second-Biggest Point Gain Ever."

Which is it? Whether a bad market or a good one, it doesn't seem to matter to the newspaper people, as long as you buy their paper.

Need a more current example?

Consider some headlines from another highly respected national business newspaper on October 15, 2002; "Back at Recession Low, Outlook Turns Dark." What would you do if you saw a headline like that? Would you mortgage the house and put everything into mutual funds that day? I don't think so.

Now read the headlines from October 16, 2002, the very next day. The market rocketed 218 points, and the paper's lead story was "Stocks Follow Through With Big, Broad Gains on Improved Earnings."

You'd be crazy to make your investment decisions based on what gets reported. Scare tactics one minute, all sunshine and roses the next. They can't even call 'em as they see 'em, so I go nuts when

---

[2] *Lowe et al. v. SEC*, 472 U.S. 181 (1985).

a client tells me someone on CNBC has "predicted" that the market will be at a certain level by next spring. What market deity whispered in their ear? These forecasts would almost be funny if they weren't so dangerous. They don't have to be dangerous to you anymore.

When the talking heads share their market wisdom with you, realize it's more an exercise in their ego flexing than in providing valuable financial advice. These people think they know what the market should be doing. They're sure of themselves and what the future holds for the markets and for share prices.

Contrary Indicator

I consider the type of advice you hear on TV as arrogant and expensive—and following it a great way to lose a bundle. Most of these market "analysts" rely on their gut feelings. They rarely refer to any hard evidence to support their views. These analysts are only sharing their sentiments—and sentiments aren't worth a lot.

"Always listen to experts. They'll tell you what can't be done and why. Then do it."
ROBERT HEINLEIN, Author

As a matter of fact, many successful advisers use so-called expert predictions as a contrary indicator.[3] Meaning, as the talking heads on TV and writers of newsletters get more bullish, these advisers—including myself—recognize this as a possible time to sell. Why? Because, according to my research, the experts are usually wrong. **In fact, relying on experts to be wrong has worked well for years. In other words, experience suggests that when the media is most optimistic about the market, stocks seem to fall.** And when the

---
[3] Hersh Shefrin, *Beyond Greed and Fear*, 60.

media acts the gloomiest, stocks have often risen. This is illustrated in the following charts, which graph the movement of the Dow Jones Industrial Average (DJIA) over more than 30 years. The boxes contain a few examples of some of the financial headlines that appeared along the way.

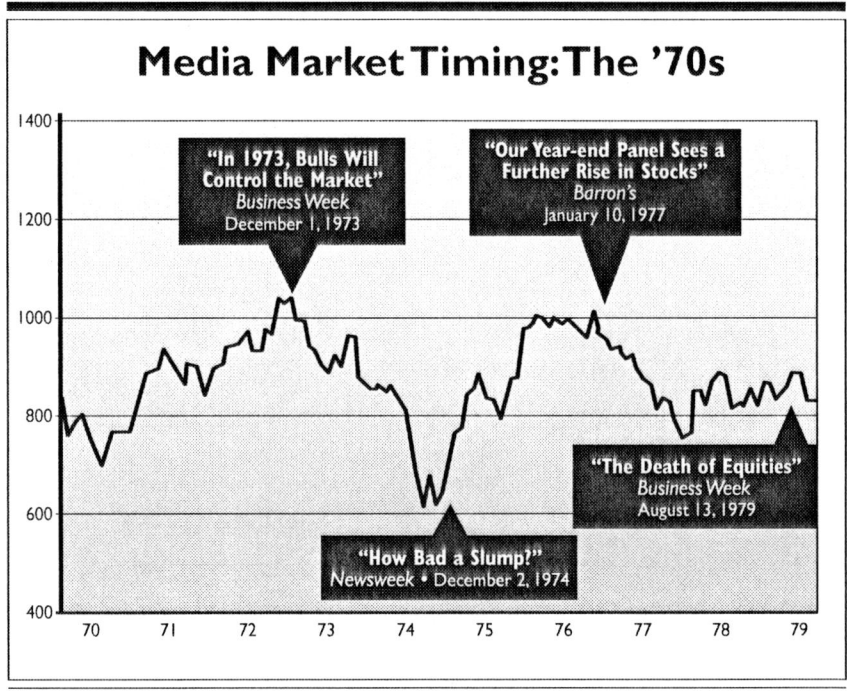

Business Week was really impressed by equities in the early 1970s. By December 1972, it told readers the market would rise through 1973. Instead, the economy fell into the worst recession in 50 years and the market tanked. By December 1974, *Newsweek* was forecasting that the slump would never end. But a few months later, it did.

In January 1977, hotshot experts assembled by *Barron's* were certain of healthy gains ahead. Investors weren't so certain and the Dow fell 21 percent over the next year.

By August 1979, we were trying to cope with double-digit interest and inflation rates. *Business Week's* cover story proclaimed "The Death of Equities." But, actually, that market set the stage for the huge bull market of the 1980s.

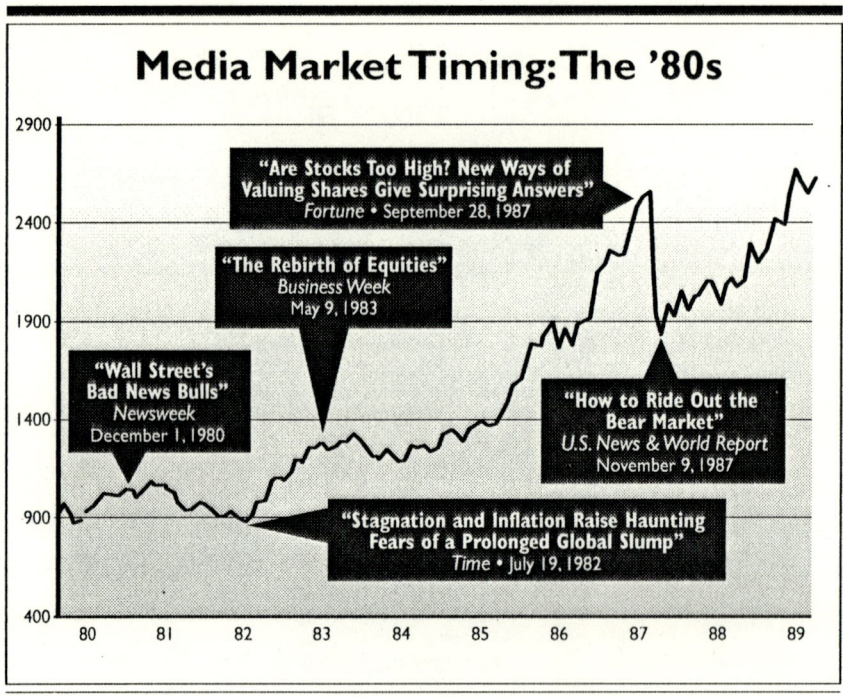

In July 1982, *Time* magazine warned us of another Great Depression. But a few weeks later, investors carried the market up 66 percent.

In May 1983, *Business Week* decided to bring the market back to life—having buried it three years prior. Its "Rebirth of Equities" was stillborn. The market shriveled by 16 percent.

The market recovered in 1984 and continued to climb into 1987. By September 1987, *Fortune* magazine became a true believer. They suggested there might be new ways to value stocks that might justify the market's high levels. Wrong again. The October 1987 crash—the worst since the Great Depression of 1929—resolved the issue.

A few months later, *U.S. News and World Report* told readers how to survive the bear market—but of course, by then the bear was gone.

If you review the accompanying charts of the 1990s and 2000s, you'll see the same pattern repeated. Time after time, the journalists got it wrong. By the mid-1990s, after the Federal Reserve raised interest rates in 1994, *Fortune* predicted a "bear market ahead." The market rallied 37 percent in the next 12 months instead.

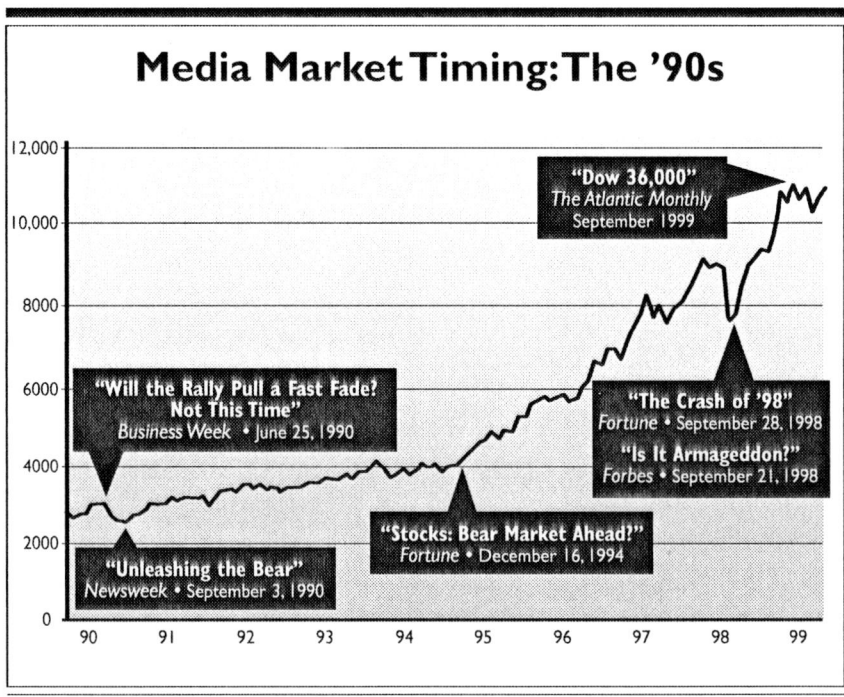

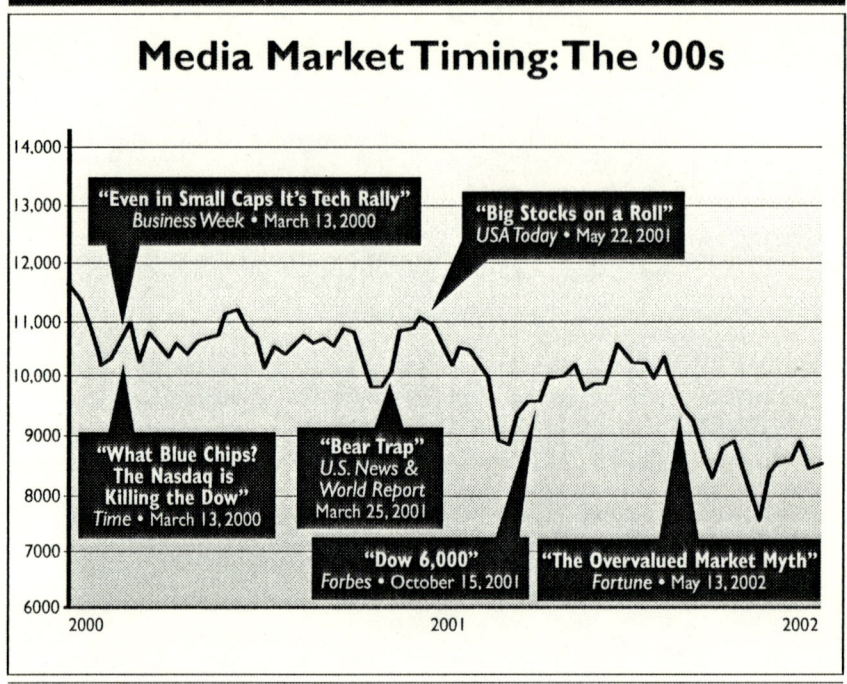

The late 1990s were great for the market. By then, many journalists were convinced the boom would never end. In September 1999, the *Atlantic Monthly* set the Dow target for 36,000.

Things didn't work out that way, unfortunately. The Dow peaked at 11,723 in mid-January 2000. (That's just a smidgen shy of 36,000.)

Pick up your newspaper or *Money* magazine right now. Look at the headlines. Do you have any reason to believe the people who wrote those articles have finally gotten it right when you consider their track record over the last 30 years?

I'm not trying to bash financial journalists, by the way. They're only doing their jobs, just as their editors are only doing their jobs, which is to sell papers. **I simply want you to understand that newspapers are in the business of selling newspapers, not of making you a successful and contented investor.** I also want you to understand the risks you take by letting the headline *du jour* affect your investment decisions.

My suggestion is to consider market predictions by experts as noise—and change the channel.

Media's Value with Regard to Individual Companies

So the media stinks when it comes to predicting the direction of the market, but surely the media is on the right track when it reports on the health of individual companies. Right?

Wrong. Very, very wrong.

People are frequently confused by news concerning a stock they own. Sometimes the company has a great report, yet the stock falls—and vice versa. Why? The simple answer is that all known information is instantly reflected in the price of a stock. By the time you read the information in the paper, it's old news.

Often, the moment this good news is officially publicized, the smart money will sell—and lock in a quick profit. However, the public starts buying *after* the news is released—at the exact time when the smart money is selling, and as the big investors sell out, the price drops.

The opposite of this can be true as well. When there are rumors of bad news, insiders and other smart money investors sell before that news is made public. In such a case, the stock price slowly drifts lower as those with inside information sell. Finally, by the time the bad news is published, the stock may already be at a low point. In this case, the smart money investors who sold earlier may come back and buy shares—at the exact time the public starts selling. **If you want to pay attention to cover stories and headlines, use them as a contrarian indicator.** Whenever you see the CEO of a company touted on the cover of *Business Week, Newsweek,* or any other nationally circulated periodical, it's probably time to sell.[4] All the good news is out, and all the people who would want to invest have already invested. There's no one left to buy—and when you have no new buyers, you have no force lifting prices or even holding prices stable. As a result, the price of the stock could plummet.

Magazines measure mass opinion: By the time a company makes a cover, the public is in love with the stock. Everyone and their cousins own shares. When no more potential buyers are out there, stocks fall.

As just one example, *Fortune* ran a photo of Cisco Systems CEO John Chambers on the front of its May 15, 2000 issue. The article began by asking readers which stock they'd want to own if they were stranded on a deserted island and could own just one. The answer: "Cisco, the stock that rose 82,000 percent in the 1990s? Yup, you've got to own Cisco."

Although the earnings numbers were on fire, the market didn't agree with *Fortune*. Cisco peaked at $82 on March 27, 2000, less than two months before the article ran, and hit bottom at $13.19 in April 2002)—a plunge of 84 percent. That's what I call an expensive magazine!

Let the market be your guide. It's much more accurate than using your judgment or listening to media noise or headlines. And never mind economic forecasts and analyses. Seriously, never mind them.

How About That Economy?

There's a lot of coverage in the press about the direction of the economy, presented as if it enlightens and forewarns investors. But does any of that matter for making money in the market?

---

[4] David Saito-Chung, "Magazine Covers Can Serve As Sell Signal," *Investor's Business Daily*, June 29, 2001, http://www.investors.com/learn/Icsell12.asp.

Peter Lynch answered this question better than I could. In case you don't know, Lynch ran Fidelity's Magellan Fund for 13 years (1977-1990). In that period, Magellan was up over 2,700 percent. In the last five years, when Magellan was the largest fund in the world, it outperformed 99 percent of all stock funds.[5]

Peter retired in 1990 at the age of 46. He is the author of various bestsellers and considered one of the true stock market wizards of our time. He once said that if you spend three minutes a year evaluating the economy, that's three minutes too long.

Peter and I agree that tracking the economy won't help you make money in the stock market. Why? Because the stock market moves 6 to 12 months ahead of the economy.[6] That means the economy could be doing horribly, and the market could do well—and vice versa. We've seen examples of that in the preceding pages. The media did get it right with regard to the economy, but the economy had nothing to do with how well the market performed.

With the exhibits from this chapter in mind, tell me: Would you have been better off by paying attention to what *Newsweek*, *Time*, the major newspapers, radio, and TV were telling you about the future, or would you have been better off to simply listen to what the market was telling you?

Clearly, if you have the tools to understand what the market is broadcasting, you'll be better off by far. That's all you have to listen to, and I'll show you how to do exactly that.

What About Significant Political Events?

Should investors sit on the sidelines while something like terrorist attacks are going on? If you want an investment strategy that will help you achieve the really important things in your life, the answer is no.

---

[5] Peter Lynch and John Rothchild, *One Up on Wall Street* (New York: Penguin USA, 1990).
[6] Martin Zweig, *Martin Zweig's Winning on Wall Street* (New York: Warner, 1997).

Let the market interpret current events, and then follow the market, as I'll show you in chapter 8 of this book.

There's always been some catastrophe that we're trying to manage and cope with. We've been through a depression, World War II, the Cuban missile crisis, and an assassinated U.S. president. We even went through September 11, 2001.

As horrific and frightening as those events were, the stock market has continued to thrive because the United States of America continues to thrive. As long as you believe America will continue to grow, even in the face of adversity, you should invest—as long as the market gives the all-clear signal.

We've always survived turmoil, and unfortunately, we'll probably always have a crisis to overcome. The current terrorist problem that the civilized world is dealing with could be with us for many years—and that's certainly a human tragedy. However, no one can revoke the business cycle. There will always be companies that make higher profits. There will always be companies continuing to expand with new products in new markets. Their share prices will increase and the people who own those shares will profit. This simple fact explains the next two exhibits.

PAY ATTENTION • Listen to the Market, Not the Media

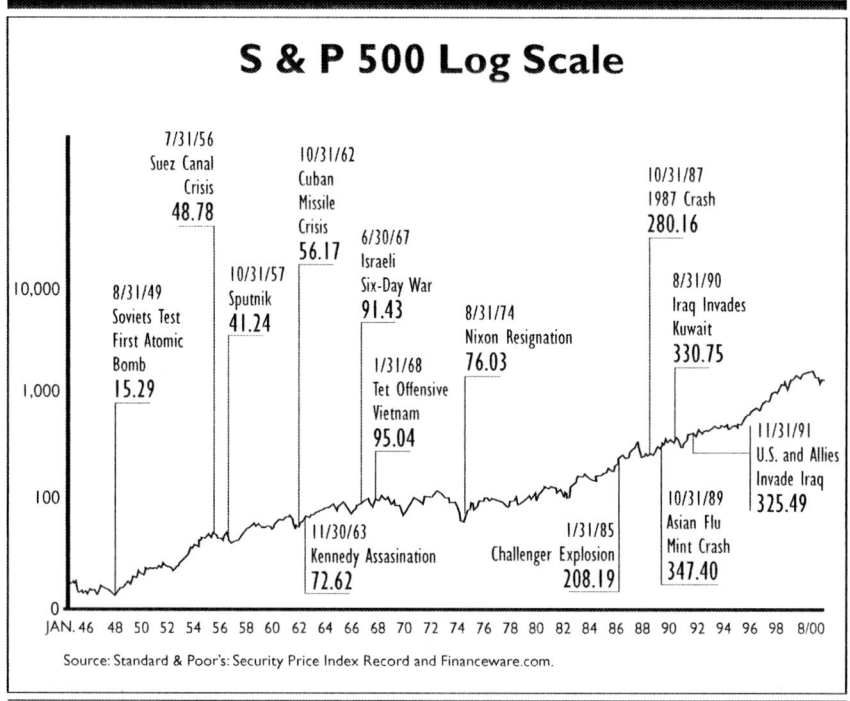

Notice how the market continued to climb—surviving everything from the attack on Pearl Harbor to 9/11/01. As bad as 9/11 was, by the end of September, the DJIA was 9.6 percent higher than it was on 9/10. In fact, the longest time it ever took for the market to recover from a catastrophe was after the attack on Pearl Harbor—six months afterward, the market was still down. On average, after a crisis, the market initially dropped 11 percent. Three months after the average crisis, the market was 9.4 percent higher than pre-crisis levels.[7]

As you can see, the stock market is resilient.

---

[7] Tim Gehner, "Will History Repeat Itself? Will the Stock Market be Resilient after the Recent Crisis?" Johnson Investment Counsel, 2003, http://www.johnsoninv.com/jol/Library/archive/crisisarticle.asp.

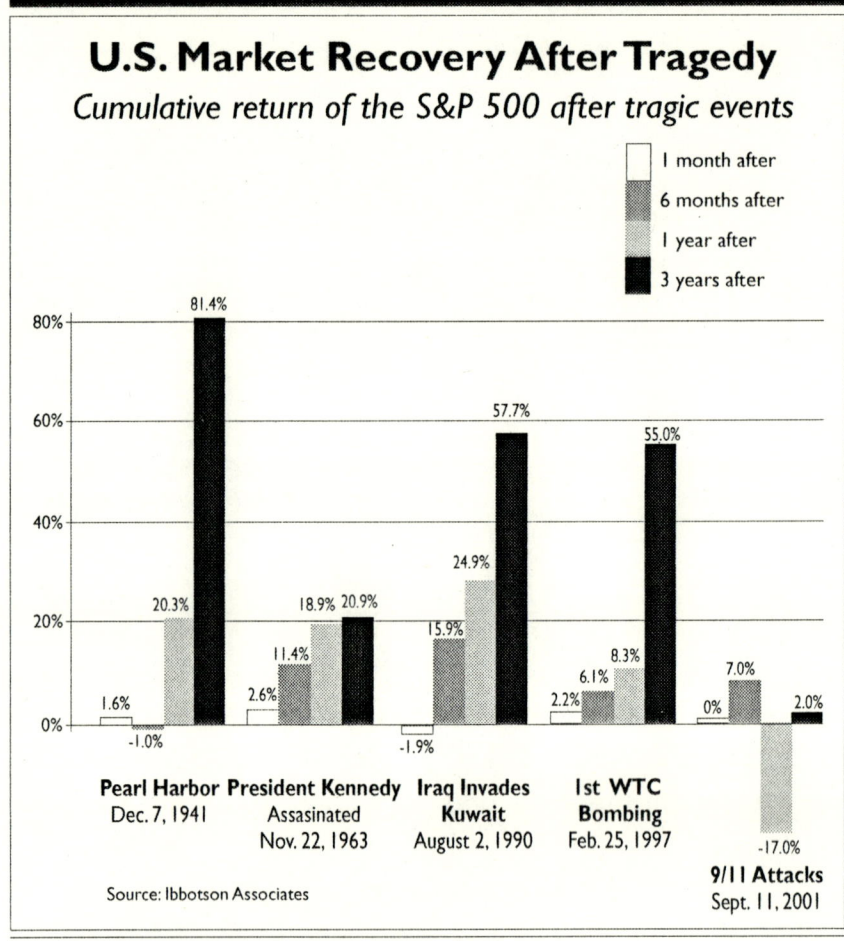

Even though the media does its best to scare you, the evidence suggests that catastrophes end up as just a blip on the radar screen. Political and military disasters have never dealt a death blow to our financial markets.

So why does the news media go to such lengths to tie world events to your money? To sell newspapers—remember, that's their mission. They have no interest in educating you or in helping you make better investment decisions.

Advertising: More Hype, More Misdirection

On par with the noise you get from the media, the hawking of investments is just as loud. The simple truth is that if you want to make good investment decisions, you have to ignore ads. They present skewed information, and investors who rely on that information often make costly mistakes, particularly in the area of mutual funds.

Why does anyone pay attention to ads in the first place? Because fund investors must select the best funds within a universe of over 10,000 choices, and they narrow their search by relying on track records—information that's found in the fund ads.

Mutual fund companies are delighted when you rely on their ads to choose your fund, because their ads often show attractive results based on a blended three- or five-year track record—and this is where the problem starts. Three- and five-year track records are miserable predictors of future results.[8]

Please don't misunderstand me. I agree that track records of mutual funds are critically important, but most investors look at the wrong time frame in making their decisions.

The name of the fund in the following example has been omitted, but it's an extremely popular fund—so popular that there's a high likelihood you own it right now.

What you see is how the fund performed year by year.

Fund A

Year	1997	1998	1999	2000	2001	6-31-02
Performance	21.86	86.61	100.57	−37.92	−34.65	−33.94

To compute Fund A's three-year performance average as of January 2000, we would add up the performance for 1997, 1998,

---

[8] Mark Hulbert, "Momentum is Fleeting: So How to Capture It in Funds?" Strategies, *New York Times*, sec. 3, July 7, 2002.

and 1999 and divide by 3, which gives us an average annual return of just under 70 percent.

If the fund ran an ad in January 2000, that ad could truthfully show an average annual return of 70 percent over the past three years. When you saw that, you'd probably say, "Wow, that's a good fund. It's got a good three-year history. I'll put some money in."

This behavior would be consistent with the conventional wisdom that tells you to buy and hold forever. You tell yourself that you can buy and hold, and eventually you'll earn at least the average rate of 70 percent per year. If you'd followed this "wisdom" and held onto this fund, you would have gotten creamed over the next three years. Assume you'd invested $100,000 on January 1, 2000.

You would have lost nearly 38 percent in 2000 (your $100,000 is now worth $62,000), 35 percent in 2001 (your $62,000 dropped to $40,300), and 34 percent for the first six months in 2002 (your $40,300 became $26,598). So relying on the historical track record can cost you a fortune—but you already know that.

And don't think that the only people who made this mistake were those who invested in this fund. Anyone who invests based on three-year track records also makes this mistake. Consider the S&P Index 500. Had you seen an ad for this index fund in January 2000, you would have seen that the average annual return was 27 percent for the trailing three-year period. Based on that, many people projected they would continue to earn 27 percent (or close to it) in the years to come. They felt comfortable investing their money.

However, had you invested based on that track record alone, you would have lost 9 percent in the year 2000, 12 percent in 2001, and 25 percent in the year 2002. These losses were mostly avoidable. How did you lose this money? Because you went the easy way and only looked at the (ancient) past, which has no bearing on the present.

Eric Tyson, a nationally syndicated columnist, did a study and found that of the funds that ranked number one in performance over the past 15 years, over the subsequent 3-, 5- and 10-year periods, 80 percent of those star funds performed worse than the average similar fund[9]. So just when the ads were telling you how great the fund was, it started underperforming.

Mark Hulbert wrote,

> Three-year track records do not do a good job of capturing momentum . . . these considerations help explain why a number of mutual fund rating services have been so disappointing, despite their use of methods that otherwise seem eminently reasonable. The best known of such services, of course, is Morningstar Inc. Although it does not rely exclusively on three-year returns in building its famous star-ranking system, it places more weight on them than for returns over any other period. Given the inadequacy of three-year track records, it should not be surprising that Morningstar's top-rated equity funds have significantly lagged the market. . . . Morningstar's top-ranked equity funds underperformed the Wilshire 5000 by an annualized average of 5.5 percentage points from the beginning of 1991 through May 31, 2002.[10]

Five and a half percent annualized is a mountain of money! For example, had you invested $100,000 over that same period and underperformed the market by 5.5 percent each year, you would be giving up *$151,000*—enough to buy a college education for all your grandchildren.[11] Following the three-year track records can be expensive.

Morningstar recently changed the way they rate mutual funds. However, they still place a great emphasis on long-term track

---

[9] Eric Tyson, "Star Funds Burn Out Quickly" *San Francisco Chronicle*, March 8, 1997.
[10] Hulbert, "Momentum is Fleeting: So How to Capture It in Funds?"
[11] Based on investing $100,000 for 125 months at 12% versus 6.5%.

records, and I doubt their own record will improve significantly in the future.

Hulbert doesn't stop there:

> Another popular mutual fund newsletter, Louis Rukeyser's *Mutual Funds*, focuses exclusively on three-year returns and has also underperformed the market. . . . The funds on the Louis Rukeyser Honor Roll have lagged the Wilshire since the beginning of 1991 by an average of 10 percentage points a year through May 31.[12]

Is your objective to own funds that were great in the past, or to make money in the present so you can achieve what's most important to you? **If your objective is to achieve financial goals, you can't rely on long-term track records.**

We know that most fund managers cannot consistently do well.[13] Those funds that do well happen to own shares of companies in a strong part of the market, and as long as that part of the market remains strong, their fund's performance will be strong. But that kind of success is fleeting, which is why so few funds have consistently good results.

We could spend a great deal of time studying why so few funds do well consistently. At the end of the day, it doesn't matter why as much as it matters that you understand this is a fact. That's all you need to know.

We have evidence to support that once a fund starts doing really well, it will probably continue doing well for another 8 to 12 months in a generally good market.[14] We also know that once a fund is past its prime, it's folly to stick with it.

---

[12] Hulbert, "Momentum is Fleeting: So How to Capture It in Funds?"
[13] Timothy Middleton, "Upgrader Funds Always Follow the Leaders," *MSN Money*, August 20, 2002, http://moneycentral.msn.com/content/p28782.asp?Printer.
[14] Timothy Middleton, "Upgrader Funds Always Follow the Leaders."

So the track record does have a lot to do with which funds to buy—but not the 3-, 5-, and 10-year track records. That history won't help you make money; you have to be much more current.

With that in mind, let's examine a few ads and how they try to pull the wool over your eyes. In the following examples, the names of the funds have been changed to protect the not-so-innocent.

Smart Talk from Hugh Jeego

What the Numbers Say

AVERAGE ANNUAL TOTAL RETURNS AS OF 12/31/99

JEEGO FUND	CATEGORY	1 YEAR	5 YEAR	LIFE OF FUND/10 YEAR*
Enterprise	Aggressive Growth	187.83%	–	217.83% (9-30-98)
Growth 20	Aggressive Growth	109.48%	–	60.36% (6-30-97)
U.S. Emerging Growth	Aggressive Growth	187.83%	–	217.83% (9-30-98)
Overseas	International	96.27%	–	61.53% (6-30-98)
Mid Cap Growth	Growth	92.02%	–	35.78% (12-31-96)
Growth	Growth	75.06%	34.86%	31.75% (12-31-93)
Total Return	Core Equity	89.75%	30.57%	19.06%*
Foreign Major Markets	International	42.39%	–	26.40% (6-30-98)
Common Stock	Growth	40.35%	24.24%	21.59%*
Blue Chip 100	Core Equity	38.88%	–	36.40% (6-30-97)
Opportunity	Growth	33.39%	23.38%	17.23%*
Growth & Income	Core Equity	32.23%	–	31.87% (12-29-95)
Small Cap Value	Growth	28.09%	–	16.58% (12-31-97)

These are very small words that you can barely read. Please consult our magic crystal ball for the legal disclosures and obfuscation.

In the preceding ad, you can see that the overseas fund returned 96 percent in one year. Since inception, the ad indicates that the fund returned on average 62 percent. If you look at the small print, you see that the fund has been around for only one and a half years. Gotcha.

This technique can easily mislead you. Often, the fund company opens up a new fund. If they do so when the market is favorable, the fund will have a stellar track record because it's not burdened by the years when the market was in the dumps. But such a "track record" is really no track record at all.

This should be considered a fund in its infancy—a baby fund that might be good for someone else to invest in, but it's not worth the risk for you.

Another technique that fools investors is to use blended long-term track records, which are meaningless. Long-term track records are skewed by the results of one or two excellent years.

Amazing.

It's no surprise Fako Funds ended 1999 with eight outstanding no-load mutual funds. Because this achievement comes from our commitment to consistently competitive performance over time. Call or visit our web site for information and you'll be amazed, too.

	AVG ANNUAL TOTAL RETURNS AS OF 12/31/99		
	ONE YEAR	FIVE YEARS	LIFE OF FUND
Fako Information Technology Fund	161.40%		88.81%
Fako Mid Cap Growth Fund	151.46%		97.03%
Fako New Generation Fund	144.20%		47.50%
Fako Small Company Growth Fund	104.39%	30.79%	27.78%
Fako Select Fund	81.68%		76.90%
Fako Growth and Income Fund	61.32%	28.28%	19.74%
Fako 100 Fund	52.28%	22.64%	19.76%
Fako Balanced Fund	44.58%		54.96%

Making It Up As We Go Along.

Here's another fund ad. Look at the Fako Small Company, sporting a 104 percent one-year return. The five-year return was 30 percent, and over the life of the fund, the average return was 27 percent.

What if I take out the best year? If, out of 10 years, I take out just one good year and then I recalculate the return over the life of the fund, the story changes: the average return of that fund drops from 27 percent to 13 percent. That's a 50 percent reduction—quite a difference.

So don't let these mutual fund companies tell you what great stock pickers they are and mislead you. One or two good years don't make a great fund. What's much more important is what's happening in the market right now and how the fund has performed in the last 12 months.

Another technique touts the expertise of the fund manager. The ad will go on and on about how talented this manager is at seeking opportunity and avoiding danger. But if the market is weak, most stocks will decline.[15] That means regardless of how great the fund manager is, the stocks held in the fund are going to decrease in value in a generally weak market.

Unfortunately, most mutual fund managers *must* stay invested in the market at all times—regardless of current market conditions. Each fund has a different set of rules set forth in its prospectus (a contract spelling out what the manager can and can't do). The prospectuses of most mutual funds direct the managers to keep at least 90 percent of your money in the market at all times—no matter how bad they think the market is, no matter how much money they think the stocks they hold are going to lose. You pay these people hefty fees, and they expose you to this type of risk. (If you don't believe me, call your fund and ask, *What percentage of the money I*

---

[15] Gerald M. Loeb, *The Battle for Investment Survival* (Burlington, VT: Fraser, 1995).

invest will always *be in the market regardless of market conditions?* The answer should make you nervous.)

If you invest in a mutual fund and think it'll protect you in bad markets, you're mistaken. Bill Gross, who manages the world's largest bond fund, is touted by the fund he works for as the best bond manager in the world. This might be true. In an interview in late 2002, Bill said he expects the next three years to be poor to mediocre for bond investors. What does Bill plan on investing in? Bonds.

Why would he buy bonds if he expects the market to be so poor? Because he has no choice. He is directed to do so as outlined by the fund's prospectus. Even though he thinks other areas might provide better investment opportunities, Bill must invest the money he manages in bonds.

Think about surfing in the ocean. If people surfed like most fund managers run funds, they'd take their board out to the same exact spot every single day regardless of what the weather and water are doing. Note to self, for fund managers: At least check the conditions before heading out to sea!

Even though your broker and fund manager fail to, I want you to check the weather reports first and then either go to the best investment spot possible or just stay home in case it's too gnarly out there. Which makes more sense to you, dude?

With all this in mind, I hope you realize you must have a method for protecting yourself when you invest in mutual funds, and that method must evaluate the strength of the market and guide your investments accordingly. Your fund manager (and in most cases, your financial adviser) won't do this for you regardless of how great the ads say she is. She keeps you exposed to the market at all times, regardless of the risk.

If you allow these people to keep you invested regardless of risk, don't be surprised to see your account values disintegrate in a bad market.

Points of Interest

- The media's mission is to sell newspapers and airtime. They don't care about how much money you make or lose. They're not interested in educating you.
- Don't look for stock market insights from your TV or from *Money* magazine. Market commentators usually rely on their own feelings about the market, and their feelings are no more predictive than yours or mine.
- The market is very good at predicting what the economy will be doing six to nine months down the road. Don't look to the economy to predict what will happen in the stock market.
- As frightening as world events can be, investors are better served by ignoring the headlines and paying attention to what the market is saying. The financial markets have recovered from every political and military catastrophe since 1925. America is resilient—and so is our business community. The market provides all the information you need to make good investments.
- Long-term track records are:
  1. Misleading because one or two great years skew the overall average return.
  2. Irrelevant because the market changes too fast. Look at the high-ranking funds as of September 2000—they were tech funds. Had you relied on those high rankings to invest, you wouldn't have enough money today to buy my book. Three-, 5- and 10-year track records have not been good indicators of future success.

(Continued on next page.)

3. Risky because fund managers must comply with the rules laid out in their prospectuses. Most prospectuses call for equity funds to be at least 90 percent invested in stocks at all times. Eventually, this will cause you to lose money. As an alternative, use my safety net method to gauge the health of the market and withdraw money from funds when the market is unhealthy or once your fund underperforms the market.

Exercises

1. List two examples of when you invested based on something you read or heard in the media.
    a. What were the circumstances?
    b. What were the results?
2. Ask yourself how you're protected against a broad market decline; after all, your mutual fund managers aren't going to do this for you. Nope, that's my mission—and we're on it.

Take Action
Generate Income with Your Investments

"You cannot escape the responsibility of tomorrow by evading it today."
ABRAHAM LINCOLN, 16th U.S. President

You are now hip to the financial sensationalism of the media, know to leave your baser emotions out of the investment selection and selling processes, and are clear about why you want to invest in the first place. No doubt you're chomping at the bit, ready to get on with it. How can you generate greater wealth and consistent income with your investments?

When most people think about investments that generate income, they first look to bonds and preferred stock, which can be attractive options for those who don't want to worry about their money and want to sleep well at night. All other things being equal, they help maintain principal and give you the required income like clockwork. Most investors love owning these investments; to some, they become a security blanket. Just knowing they own bonds and preferred stock makes them feel they're avoiding the uncertainty inherent in the market. They're placating their fear.

Emotionally, this may make sense, and for some it's the smartest financial move they could make. But if you're like most people, investing all your money in fixed income securities could be a huge mistake—and one that's totally avoidable. Why is it a mistake? Because, over time, people who own these types of investments and nothing else can lose it all.

Assume you need $35,000 from your investments each year to maintain your retirement lifestyle. If you have $600,000 in bonds and earn 6 percent each year, the interest will generate $36,000.

Congratulations, you have it made—this year. But how long are you planning to be retired?

What about the next decade? In 10 years, you'll still be earning $36,000 every year. But how much will you need to maintain your lifestyle then? Are health care, prescription drugs, or travel going to be cheaper 10 years from now?

You can see where I'm going with this. When you retire, your income may stay fixed, but your expenses won't. They'll keep going up. Let's assume that over 10 years, inflation averaged just 2 percent. The retiree who had it made on $36,000 a year when he retired would then need $43,900 a year just to get by because of this miserly 2 percent inflation. Where would that extra income come from?

Either this person would have to go back to work, rely on charity or family, cut her standard of living, or spend her capital. Do you think she really wants to be the "friendly face" upselling fries at the drive-through window? Ouch!

If you rely on fixed income, nonstop inflation seals your fate. In most cases, fixed income investors have a high chance of running out of money during their lifetime. This spells (you already know this) Flippy Burger. Inflation and bad investments are the reasons Americans are going back to work after retirement.

It's possible, though, to be sitting pretty and not even know it. If you have the right investments, you can generate enough income that you'll never have to set foot in a fast-food restaurant unless you're looking for a quick meal. At a seminar many years ago, I met a woman named Stella who had recently become a widow. While her husband was still alive and running a successful business, she saved and invested more than $2 million in an investment account. During his lifetime, she invested this money for growth and continued to rely on her husband's income to provide for the family's daily needs.

Then things changed. The business ran into trouble, and her husband became so desperate that he failed to pay his life insurance premiums. Then he died.

The business had no value without him. He had no life insurance for his wife to collect. Still, Stella had her home and the $2 million investment account.

I was amazed when I met this woman, because even though she had $2 million in investments, she had no idea how to convert those assets into investments that would generate the income she needed. Rather than use her assets to make ends meet, she tried to cut her expenses by disconnecting her cable TV service and canceling her tennis club affiliation.

I showed her how to take her existing assets and create the income she wanted. Once she understood how to convert equity growth into current income from her investments—without buying bonds—she began to live again.

Stella didn't understand the rules, and as a result, didn't understand how to use her assets wisely. When you play a game and misunderstand the rules, you usually lose, which is the fate of most investors.

So what are the real rules you need to understand if you're interested in generating income for a secure future? Take a look at the following exhibit. This chart summarizes the results of various portfolios, withdrawal rates, and the chances of the portfolio providing income without self-destructing over a period of years.

In the left column you can see a few different portfolios, one being all bonds, another being all equities, and a few different mixes of bonds and equities in between. Focus on the right half of the chart, because that's where the numbers are adjusted for inflation.

Portfolio Success Rates 1946–1995

Withdrawal rate as a percentage of initial portfolio value

PAYOUT PERIOD	UNADJUSTED						ADJUSTED FOR INFLATION AND DEFLATION*					
	3%	4%	6%	8%	10%	12%	3%	4%	6%	8%	10%	12%
100% Stocks												
15 years	100	100	100	100	86	64	100	100	91	70	55	34
20 years	100	100	100	97	61	42	100	100	75	53	33	24
25 years	100	100	100	88	45	38	100	100	70	46	30	30
30 years	100	100	100	90	52	38	100	95	68	41	34	15
75% Stocks/25% Bonds												
15 years	100	100	100	100	86	53	100	100	95	68	46	27
20 years	100	100	100	97	48	32	100	100	75	51	27	12
25 years	100	100	100	85	42	27	100	100	65	37	22	2
30 years	100	100	100	81	48	29	100	98	68	34	7	0
50% Stocks/50% Bonds												
15 years	100	100	100	100	78	42	100	100	93	64	32	13
20 years	100	100	100	94	39	13	100	100	75	33	10	0
25 years	100	100	100	69	19	0	100	100	57	20	0	0
30 years	100	100	100	48	10	0	100	95	51	5	0	0
25% Stocks/75% Bonds												
15 years	100	100	100	100	53	17	100	100	89	50	18	7
20 years	100	100	100	68	13	3	100	100	47	16	4	0
25 years	100	100	100	15	0	0	100	93	24	4	0	0
30 years	100	100	100	0	0	0	100	71	20	0	0	0
100% Bonds												
15 years	100	100	100	72	33	11	100	100	71	21	16	9
20 years	100	100	94	29	10	0	100	90	20	12	2	0
25 years	100	100	54	12	0	0	100	46	15	2	0	0
30 years	100	100	10	0	0	0	80	(20)	12	0	0	0

NOTE: Numbers rounded to the nearest whole percentage. The number of overlapping 15-year payout periods from 1946 to 1995, inclusively, is 36; 20-year periods, 31; 25-year periods, 26; 30-year periods, 21. Stocks are represented by Standard and Poor's 500 Index, and bonds are represented by long-term., high-grade corporates. *Values based on the consumer price index.
Source: Phillip Cooley, Carl Hubbard, Daniel Walz, based on data from Ibbotson Associates.

Across the top you'll see different rates of withdrawal. The numbers on the chart indicate how likely it was historically that you were able to make withdrawals depending on the mix between stocks and bonds, the rate at which you withdrew income, and how many years you continued to draw income from the account.

If you go down to the bottom right section, for example, you can see what happened to bond investors. Assume the bond-holders wanted a 4 percent withdrawal rate adjusted for inflation for 30 years. A portfolio made up 100 percent of bonds was able to survive only 20 percent of the time. What happened the other 80 percent of the time? Can you say *Flippy Burger?* That's right. Hi ho, hi ho, it's back to work you go! Look out, Junior, Dad and Mom are moving in!

Why Bonds Are Not a Magic Bullet

Why didn't the bonds work? Because of inflation. If your income stays the same and your cost of living goes up, sooner or later you *will* go broke. If your income isn't enough to cover your needs, at some point you'll dip into your capital to make up the difference. As you deplete the capital slowly, you have less money working for you. As a result of having less capital earning a return, you have less income. So, in this scenario, your investments earn less interest, yet your cost of living continues to rise. The pace at which you spend capital increases until you're spending all capital rather than earnings, and sooner or later you're out of money.

Still don't think this could really happen to you? It happened to Dr. Mike, a retired dentist I know. He retired in 1999 with $200,000 in his IRA account. After his retirement, he started withdrawing $20,000 a year from the account, which was the equivalent of a 10 percent withdrawal rate and much too high. The market turned ugly, and Dr. Mike burned through his nest egg. Three years later, his retirement assets totaled less than $60,000 and the retired doctor now parks cars to supplement his income. (This is performed by a professional dentist on a fixed income. Don't try this at home.) Don't let it happen to you!

Equities Can Help

Look back at our chart. If you invested 50 percent of your money in bonds and the other 50 percent in equity, and you withdrew 4 percent annually adjusted for inflation over a 30-year period, you had a 95 percent chance of not running out of money. **As your time** frame expands and your withdrawal rate increases, you have a much higher likelihood of surviving financially if you invest at least a portion of your assets in equities.

There are a few key exceptions. If a person is at a certain age and reasonably doesn't expect to live much longer, she may rightfully be interested in current income without being concerned about inflation. In this case, bonds might be the way to go. If you look closely at the preceding exhibit, you'll see that if your life expectancy was 25 years, and you needed to take out only 3 percent of your capital or less (and you didn't have a concern about leaving money to Junior), bonds might be the way to go because, historically, this scenario has 100 percent survivability. But I don't recommend a 100 percent fixed-income, pure-bond portfolio for many people. I think you can already see why.

Keep in mind that the portfolio success rates chart is based on the past. It would be a huge mistake to invest solely on the basis of this report, since the past is absolutely no guarantee of the future.

These are the long-term rules of the game, so I wouldn't suggest that anyone rely simply on this chart—don't plunk down your life savings in an equity fund and expect to sit and watch the checks roll in over the next 30 years. You need to understand the short-term rules of investing and how they relate to the long-term rules to achieve your financial goals.

"He who wishes to be rich in a day will be hanged in a year."
LEONARDO DA VINCI, Artist, Inventor, and Scientist

The Rules of Equity Investment

Let's clarify the long-term rules. The following chart shows that if you had invested a dollar in small company stocks in 1925, it would have grown to $7,800 by 2001—beating all the alternatives.

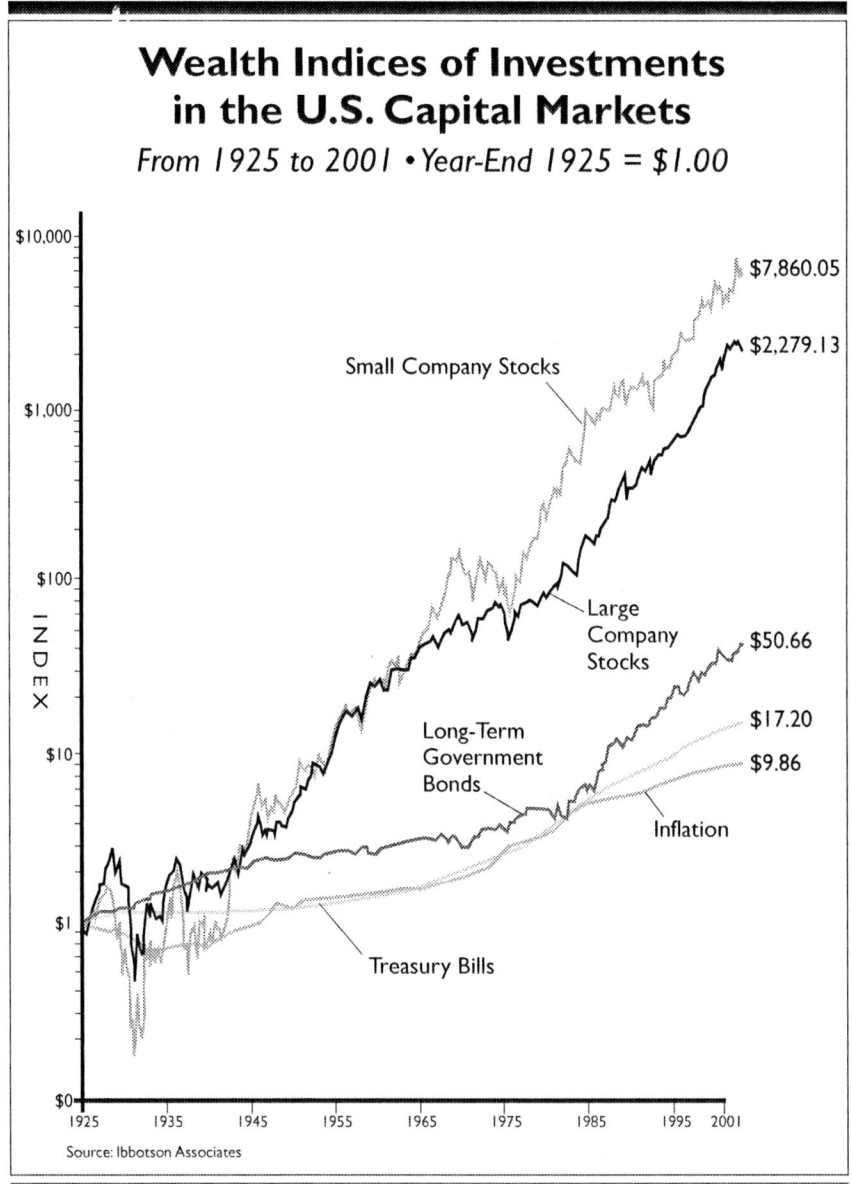

Wealth Indices of Investments in the U.S. Capital Markets
From 1925 to 2001 • Year-End 1925 = $1.00

Source: Ibbotson Associates

What made the market go up over this long time frame?

It was Darwinist capitalism: Companies that provide a service or product valued by consumers thrive. They sell their goods at a profit, then take those profits and invest the money to build more efficient factories so they can provide their goods at lower prices to beat their competition. Those who provide the greatest value in products and services become more and more profitable, and those profits help those companies become larger and even more profitable. As the companies become more profitable, the value of the company grows, and that's reflected in a greater share price. It's a cycle of success.

Take a look at the next chart. It tracks earnings of the S&P 500 companies and their share prices. You can see that over the long term, there's a very strong correlation between earnings and share prices.

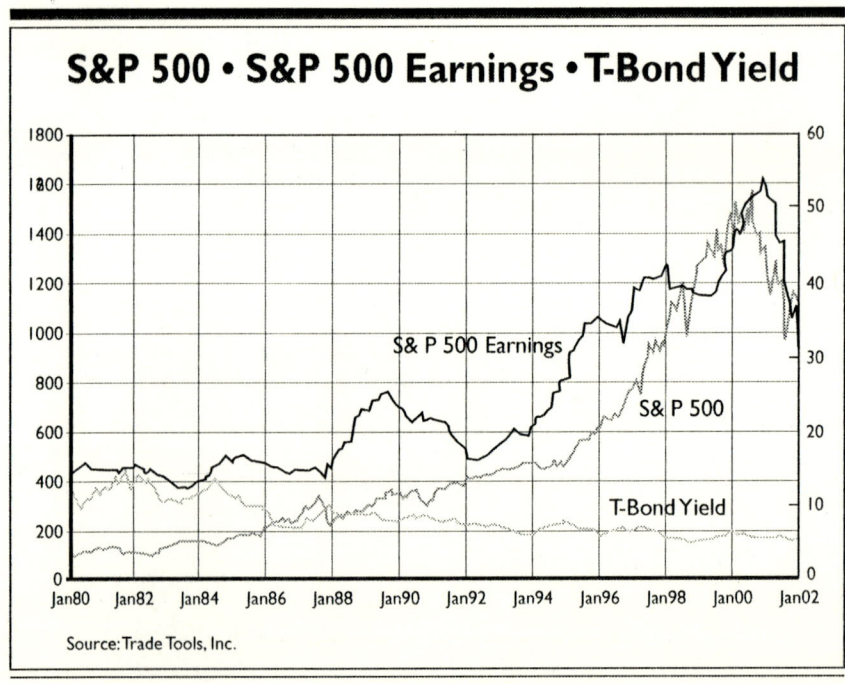

As the stockbrokers intone, if you believe in freedom and capitalism, you should believe in the stock market over the long run. But, as the economist Milton Friedman astutely commented, in the long run, we're all dead.

With that cheerful observation in mind, we must also look at the short run and consider how that affects us, too. What causes the market to gyrate on a day-to-day basis? Think of the stock market's short-term performance as a farmer's market. How are tomatoes priced at the farmer's market? It depends on three things: how many people are selling tomatoes, how many tomatoes they're trying to sell, and how many tomato buyers show up. Over the short run, the quality of the tomatoes isn't that important. You may have the reddest, most succulent tomatoes in the world. If it rains on market day and only a handful of buyers show up, the price is going to plummet.

If, on the other hand, you have nothing but splotchy, overripe fruit, but you're the only one who has tomatoes for sale, and you arrive at the market on Tomato Festival Day, you won't have any problem selling your rotten harvest at top prices.

Same thing with stocks. Even if you own great stocks, if you can't find any buyers for shares in the companies you own, you'll have to drop the price until somebody is lured into buying. In a bear market (like the farmer's market glutted with tomato sellers), you'll have trouble getting good prices for even the best stocks.

So in the long run, freedom, capitalism, and earnings propel the general market skyward. But in the short run, the market does the twist—it's full of ups and downs and all-arounds.

Be Sure You Apply the Right Rules for Your Situation

Problems occur when people take their long-term rule book (stocks go up over time), apply it to the short term, get disappointed, and lose money.

How do investors generally cope with disappointment? Some take their marbles, go home, and refuse to play anymore—they buy bonds instead. From an emotional standpoint, I can certainly understand such an approach. Why subject yourself to the pain, anguish, and uncertainty of the stock market? In fact, why would *anybody* do this?

The reason people invest in the unpredictable market is that they must. **Given the available options, equity investing is about the best chance you have of not spending your golden years at the golden arches.**

---

*"Courage is rarely reckless or foolish. . . .
Courage usually involves a highly realistic estimate
of the odds that must be faced."*
MARGARET TRUMAN, Author

If you have long-term goals, it makes sense to invest in equities. But let's be clear: I'm not saying you should invest in just any equities, and I'm not suggesting you invest in equities all the time, or that you invest all your money in equities. I am saying equities have a great track record of creating wealth. It just doesn't make sense to ignore that potential source of wealth and income.

When you look at the returns for small cap and large cap stocks versus bonds and inflation, you have to be impressed with equities' returns. Examine the following exhibit.

Compound Annual Rates of Return by Decade (in percent)

	1920s*	1930s	1940s	1950s	1960s	1970s	1980s	1990s	2000s**	1992–01
Large Company	19.2	–0.1	9.2	19.4	7.8	5.9	17.5	18.2	–10.5	12.9
Small Company	–4.5	1.4	20.7	16.9	15.5	11.5	15.8	15.1	8.8	15.6
Long-Term Corporate	5.2	6.9	2.7	1.0	1.7	6.2	13.0	8.4	11.8	8.1
Long-Term Government	5.0	4.9	3.2	–0.1	1.4	5.5	12.6	8.8	12.2	8.7
Immediate-Term Government	4.2	4.6	1.8	1.3	3.5	7.0	11.9	7.2	10.1	6.7
Treasury Bills	3.7	0.6	0.4	1.9	3.9	6.3	8.9	4.9	4.9	4.6
Inflation	–1.1	–2.0	5.4	2.2	2.5	7.4	5.1	2.9	2.5	2.5

*Based on the period 1925–1929
**Based on the period 2000–2001
Source: Ibbottson Associates

You can see that the *only* investment that handily beat inflation from the 1940s through the 1970s was equity. That means that if you held bonds during that period, you lost money. Your income went down relative to your expenses. During the 1980s and 1990s, inflation was tame, but equity was still the best investment.

What makes equity returns even more remarkable over this period is that we've had stock market crashes and bull markets. We had depressions and great stock market booms. We've had global war, the use of nuclear weapons, the cold war, terrorism—all kinds of horrific events.

We had deflation in the 1930s and hyperinflation in the 1970s. High interest rates and low interest rates. Republicans and Democrats. Yet the stock market continued to reward investors who were willing to take acceptable risks, despite all these catastrophes. Flip back to the graph on page 57 in chapter 3 to see how strong equities have been over long periods of time. You can see why almost any professional you talk to tries to convince you to invest in equity.

Now, I could write about how great equities are until I have chronic writer's cramp. I could show you all the charts and graphs in the world. It wouldn't convince you to invest in equities if you opened your account statements earlier today and realized the market had just erased 70 percent of the money you were planning on using to buy your vacation home.

I understand that, and I certainly hope today wasn't one of those days. Furthermore, I promise to show you tools you can use to help prevent such a drastic calamity from happening to you. (Remember selling discipline?)

Portfolio Success Rates 1946–1995

Withdrawal rate as a percentage of initial portfolio value

PAYOUT PERIOD	UNADJUSTED						ADJUSTED FOR INFLATION AND DEFLATION*					
	3%	4%	6%	8%	10%	12%	3%	4%	6%	8%	10%	12%
100% Stocks												
15 years	100	100	100	100	86	64	100	100	91	70	55	34
20 years	100	100	100	97	61	42	100	100	75	53	33	24
25 years	100	100	100	88	45	38	100	100	70	46	30	30
30 years	100	100	100	90	52	38	100	95	68	41	34	15
75% Stocks/25% Bonds												
15 years	100	100	100	100	86	53	100	100	95	68	46	27
20 years	100	100	100	97	48	32	100	100	75	51	27	12
25 years	100	100	100	85	42	27	100	100	65	37	22	2
30 years	100	100	100	81	48	29	100	98	68	34	7	0
50% Stocks/50% Bonds												
15 years	100	100	100	100	78	42	100	100	93	64	32	13
20 years	100	100	100	94	39	13	100	100	75	33	10	0
25 years	100	100	100	69	19	0	100	100	57	20	0	0
30 years	100	100	100	48	10	0	100	(95)	51	5	0	0
25% Stocks/75% Bonds												
15 years	100	100	100	100	53	17	100	100	89	50	18	7
20 years	100	100	100	68	13	3	100	100	47	16	4	0
25 years	100	100	100	15	0	0	100	93	24	4	0	0
30 years	100	100	100	0	0	0	100	71	20	0	0	0
100% Bonds												
15 years	100	100	100	72	33	11	100	100	71	21	16	9
20 years	100	100	94	29	10	0	100	90	20	12	2	0
25 years	100	100	54	12	0	0	100	46	15	2	0	0
30 years	100	100	10	0	0	0	80	20	12	0	0	0

NOTE: Numbers rounded to the nearest whole percentage. The number of overlapping 15-year payout periods from 1946 to 1995, inclusively, is 36; 20-year periods, 31; 25-year periods, 26; 30-year periods, 21. Stocks are represented by Standard and Poor's 500 Index, and bonds are represented by long-term, high-grade corporates. *Values based on the consumer price index.
Source: Phillip Cooley, Carl Hubbard, Daniel Walz, based on data from Ibbotson Associates.

More important, I hope you can see that after inflation, and with a clear set of rules for getting into and out of the market, equity becomes even more obviously the best alternative.

Let's take another look at the various portfolios chart (at left). Just to ensure that you get the picture about how *not* to outstrip your portfolio's income-producing potential, let's review the earlier example where you had a portfolio made up of 50 percent equity and 50 percent bonds, and you withdrew 4 percent of the capital every year, adjusted for inflation. Let's further assume that you withdrew the money over 30 years.

Under those conditions, looking back to 1945, you ran out of money 5 percent of the time, but 95 percent of the time your money lasted.

Since 1925, the stock market has returned 11 percent per year on average. If that's the case, how could you ever run out of money if you withdrew only 4 percent? Because the market fluctuated more in some years than in others. Also, sometimes inflation is greater than at other times.

So I'll repeat myself: As good as equity sounds, please don't make the mistake of investing *all* your money in equities and staying fully invested.

If you do this, you run the risk of experiencing . . .

The Flaw of Averages

Some investors look at the preceding chart and determine that they should invest all their money in the market all the time. Their advisers concur and rely on the law of averages to prove their point.

Pat Sullivan, founder of Scenarios Now software, calls such thinking the *flaw* of averages. Why? Let's look at an example. John and Mary have $1 million in investments. They want $80,000 in income per year. Assume they have a crystal ball. It tells them with absolute certainty that during the next 25 years, the market will average 12 percent per year. But it doesn't tell them how the market will perform on a year-to-year basis.

They invest the money in an index fund and set up systematic withdrawals of 8 percent ($80,000) per year to provide for their income. In concept, they should maintain their principal, live off the interest, and put a little away. They should go off to live a happy life in retirement.

What's wrong with this picture? Let's fast-forward 25 years. You meet John and Mary on the street—living in a refrigerator box. They've been there since last year, when they ran out of money. What happened? Did they spend foolishly? Did they change their investment strategy? Did they have health issues or other emergencies that forced additional spending?

Actually, everything went according to plan. The market averaged 12 percent for the past 25 years, exactly as the crystal ball predicted. John and Mary restricted their distributions to 8 percent of their capital, just as planned.

Here's the problem. During the first few years after they retired, returns were below 12 percent; this is the killer. The systematic withdrawal of $80,000 caused them to dip into principal—a loss from which they would never recover. Over time, they would either have to reduce their income, change their strategy, or run out of money. The following chart graphically illustrates this problem, which is again a matter of looking at the long run when the short run needs to be considered, too. Look at the far right column. This column represents what would happen to John and Mary's $1 million if the market returns are 12 percent each and every year. As you can see, John and Mary live happily ever after earning 12 percent and withdrawing 8 percent. But markets don't behave this way. In the short run, they're more volatile.

Now look at the historical returns. This is a blow-by-blow report of what really happened to their money every year. You can see that in this particular example, John and Mary were reduced to pushing a shopping cart up and down the street within 16 years (and this example doesn't even consider inflation). Why? Because the market was weak *in the first few years* after they began their withdrawals. They got caught up in the flaw of averages and ignored what was happening in the real world. They paid a heavy price.

Year	Actual Yearly Return	12% Yearly Return
1962	832,700.000	1,040,000.000
1963	940,155.600	1,082,400.000
1964	1,010,221.243	1,127,416.000
1965	1,023,825.207	1,175,287.760
1966	813,996.953	1,226,281.586
1967	972,780.086	1,280,693.451
1968	984,261.711	1,338,852.481
1969	803,193.818	1,401,124.870
1970	733,176.771	1,467,918.248
1971	735,838.725	1,539,686.583
1972	767,398.933	1,616,935.662
1973	543,085.182	1,700,229.232
1974	285,649.823	1,790,195.869
1975	274,428.860	1,887,536.676
1976	218,186.892	1,993,033.899
1977	77,403.669	2,107,560.574
1978	Broke	2,232,091.327
1979	Broke	2,367,714.476
1980	Broke	2,515,645.568
1981	Broke	2,677,242.552
1982	Broke	2,854,022.760
1983	Broke	3,047,681.925
1984	Broke	3,260,115.484
1985	Broke	3,493,442.421
1986	Broke	3,750,031.983
1987	Broke	4,032,533.586
1988	Broke	4,343,910.315
1989	Broke	4,687,476.433
1990	Broke	5,066,939.390
1991	Broke	5,486,446.877
1992	Broke	5,950,639.504

(Continued on next page.)

Year	Actual Yearly Return	12% Yearly Return
1993	Broke	6,464,709.817
1994	Broke	7,034,468.375
1995	Broke	7,666,417.761
1996	Broke	8,367,835.468
1997	Broke	9,146,866.728
1998	Broke	10,012,628.470
1999	Broke	10,975,325.750
2000	Broke	12,046,382.160
2001	Broke	13,238,585.860

Source: Pat Sullivan, Scenario Now

What's the lesson? When you're making withdrawals from investments, looking at average returns can be nice, but at best they're meaningless, and at worst they lead to potentially critical mistakes in strategy.

You can't buy and hold and forget about your investments. You may experience a very attractive *average return* over many years. But if you experience bad markets in the first few years of retirement, you may find yourself out of retirement and working faster than you can say, "Would you like fries with that?"

Gilding the Lily

At the risk of sounding like a broken record, I'll return to my harangue against buy and hold. I just demonstrated how dangerous this strategy can be. Then why do so many "professionals" advocate it? One reason is that the buy-and-forget-about-it strategy helps many fancy financial advisers make huge salaries, as you'll learn in chapter 5. And I can see why. After all, the strategy is *sooooooo* complicated. As my limited thinking can understand it, here are the basic steps:

TAKE ACTION • Generate Income with Your Investments

1. You buy something.
2. You don't sell it.
3. You totally ignore what's happening in the world, especially in the market and to your money.
4. You receive a large dose of the antidepressant *du jour* to help cope with step 3.

How do these smarty-pants advisers sell you on this? They show you the chart on page 75 (the one showing long-term results since 1925). The investment industry uses these long-term growth charts—known as *mountain charts*—as a method to lure you into their dark world. The charts show a mountain of wealth building over the decades. How can an investor argue with that? "Don't you want to take advantage of this compounding?" they ask you. "Don't you believe in America?"

These charts clearly "prove" that if you just invest your money and forget it for 40 years, you'll be a multimillionaire! Or do they?

People invest using long-term rules, but they have to deal with short-term expectations and needs. It's well worth it to buy and hold when the market goes up. How about when the market goes down? How about when the market goes down for three years straight and you need to make withdrawals? Sooner or later, you're going to jettison the buy-and-forget-about-it strategy; you're no dummy. When you do, you need an alternative that makes sense. Indeed, the buy-and-forget-about-it strategy was never a sound one to start with.

You need a methodology to protect yourself from bad markets and to help you take advantage of good opportunities as they present themselves.

Creating Income from Equity

You've seen that you can't rely on bonds or equity 100 percent of the time if you want a worry-free retirement. But I understand that investment decisions are rarely made from a purely logical perspective. I know that part of you is scared to death of equities, and part of you wants a simple, straightforward answer: Do this, and do this always. I also know that you hate to lose money. When you do, you feel that your investment methods must be wrong and you look for "a better mousetrap." But the truth is, markets change and, as a result, risk changes. You faced in chapter 2 that there is no reward without risk. Sooner or later, you'll lose money, and the trick is minimizing those losses. Minimizing your losses—and maximizing your gains, of course—requires more than the four-step buy-and-forget-about-it method. This is the central message of this book: **I unequivocally warn you against buying and holding equities indefinitely, and I wholeheartedly endorse equities as an important** *part* **of your overall investment strategy.** In other words, no to buy and hold, yes to equities, but only sometimes.

To get clear on why it's "only sometimes," and I can't give you an "always" answer, put yourself in the shoes of your Uncle Leo, who retired in 1970 and was fully invested in equity funds. Leo didn't plan on going back to work by 1974. He was looking forward to a carefree retirement, living from investment returns. But in this example, by 1974 Leo's nest egg of $100,000 shrank by more than 35 percent because of the ferocious bear market. Because his capital vanished, his income of $5,000 per year dropped to $3,500. Leo is staring at reduced income and capital reserves. All the graphs and mountain charts in the world aren't going to help Leo sleep at night. He's going to be calling you in the middle of the night with his worries.

For most individuals, the pressure and stress would be tremendous during such times. Think of all the grief Leo gets from his spouse! At some point, under these circumstances, most investors would cave in, and Leo is no exception. He'll change his investment strategy (probably put all the money in CDs) or go back to work—or both. Either way, Leo, like most buy-and-hold investors, is miserable.

If the mission of investing is to stop worrying and start enjoying the things that really matter (remember the values discussion of chapter 1?), such an investment strategy has utterly failed. It was great in theory, but no one lives in theory. We have to deal with the real world.

You probably know many investors like Leo who threw in the towel on equity investing at exactly the wrong time, despite having a great plan. The reason is that their methodology failed to protect them and created more fear. They needed an investment method that reduced stress—not one that created more. And as you'll see, by investing in a way that takes into account what's happening in the market in real time, you can reduce stress significantly.

The Bottom Line on Equities

Be sure to check with your financial adviser and be aware that your own financial situation is unique. But all things being equal, the best way to avoid going broke during retirement is to have an equity component in your portfolio when appropriate.

One way to generate income from your equity investments and ensure that you don't strip the principal is by adjusting your withdrawals to your investments' performance. For example, take 4 percent of the balance of your funds at the end of each year. If you want monthly income, you could take one-twelfth of that 4 percent every month. Let's assume you invested $100,000 at the start of one year and it grew to $120,000 by the end of that year. You'd withdraw 4 percent of the ending value or $4,800. Each month, you'd take one-twelfth of $4,800, or $400.

Using this technique, if the market lost money one year, you'd take out less money. As the market improved, you'd withdraw more money. I've seen this approach work for many people for two reasons: (1) It reduces the distributions during lean times, which is less of a drain on the capital, and during good years, income goes up. This makes financial sense. And (2) it's even more emotionally satisfying for people to use this plan because people don't like to see their capital dwindle in bad markets. For those who don't bury their heads in the sand, this technique gives them the feeling they can do something about reality rather than ignore it.

From a cash-flow perspective, though, this approach can be tough. Your expenses may be the same or increase every year, regardless of what the market happens to be doing. **The bottom line is that this approach works better if the money you withdraw is somewhat discretionary and you don't actually rely on every penny you receive.** If you can live with less money in some years, and if it feels better to maintain your capital during bad markets, this might be an excellent approach for you.

Yet it provides no shelter for investors in stormy markets. You remain exposed to the market—and to fear—regardless of the risk, and as a result, your chances of sticking with this plan for the long term are low. If the market tanks just as you implement this plan, your long-awaited retirement will be short-lived. Thank you, and have a nice day.

The best way I know to create lifetime income is to invest in equity using a safety net strategy, such as the one I outline beginning on page 163. With that in place, you can use the adjusted withdrawal method explained above.

Basically, the idea behind a safety net strategy is to invest when opportunity is greatest and retreat from investing when risk is greatest. Sound like a plan? It is—a great one that you can implement, either on your own or with the help of a competent financial adviser.

TAKE ACTION • *Generate Income with Your Investments*

Points of Interest

- Bond investing can create a false sense of security for many investors. You may have short-term peace of mind, but long term you may be flirting with catastrophe. The main cause for this is inflation.
- Before making an investment plan, understand that you're an emotional being and your emotions are very powerful—particularly fear. You can temper the impact of your emotions if you invest in a way that considers what's really happening in the market rather than trying to ignore it. To do this, use a safety net approach.
- Equity can be a very powerful way to create retirement income. But because you can't control the market, don't blindly invest in equities. Only invest in them when risk is low—and don't hold onto them forever. As you'll see, there are times when you're far better off being out of the market.
- It's critical to understand the realistic consequences of your decisions. If you need to create income from your investments for more than 25 years and you need to withdraw more than 3 percent every year, you're playing with fire if you don't use equity investments at least some of the time for some portion of your assets.

Exercises

1. What is your expected retirement date?
2. How much money will you need every month to live when you retire?
3. How much of that income will have to come from your investments?
4. How long will you need to generate that monthly income?
5. What is the rate at which you will withdraw money from your investments?

Be Selective
Know How Advisers Work (You Over)

*"The louder he talked of his honor,
the faster we counted our spoons."*
RALPH WALDO EMERSON, Essayist and Poet

Do you need an adviser to help you use what you'll learn in this book? Perhaps not, but maybe you'll want to find someone who can handle the implementation of the strategy and be both a sounding board and a source of good advice. Having a financial professional working for you could very well be the cornerstone to creating more peace of mind: He or she could take away numerous money management tasks that might easily eat up your time and keep you from doing other, more important things in life.

Of course, if you plan to work with such a person, you need to find one who's both competent and trustworthy. To do this, you need to understand the motivation of advisers and the world in which they operate. **And make no mistake; the type of adviser you work with will have a tremendous impact on the advice you receive, the investments in your portfolio, and ultimately, how successful you are in achieving your life goals.** (However, if you're unable to find an adviser who protects you from bad markets and takes advantage of good opportunities, you're better off managing your money yourself).

The financial services industry isn't so different from the medical profession. Let's assume your back hurts. What treatment advice might you get from a surgeon? An operation. From a chiropractor? Adjustments. From a traditional Chinese doctor? Acupuncture and herbs. From a western family doctor? Rest and a painkiller. Same problem, different practitioners, different prescriptions. Which one's "right"? Hard to say. Maybe all of them. Or maybe your back pain would best be resolved by one particular treatment—and exacerbated by another. As the patient, how are you supposed to know? This dilemma parallels the one you'll find when choosing a financial practitioner, because there are many different kinds. Let's take a look at some of the choices.

The Insurance Agent

First, there are the insurance-licensed individuals. People who sell insurance must be licensed by their state's insurance commission. Insurance products are sold almost exclusively on a commission basis. People who sell insurance often call themselves estate planners, but they can just be salespeople with a financial product. They could be far more interested in their commissions than in your financial well-being.

Don't let the license fool you. Each state has its own requirements for obtaining an insurance license, and it's not always so difficult to get one. In the state of California, for example, it takes about 15 hours to study and pass an easy multiple-choice test. In other words, the kid who's changing your oil today could be doing your "estate planning" next weekend.

Are you loaded up with life insurance and annuities? If so, chances are good that you get advice from an insurance agent. Insurance agents usually have no experience with any other investment alternative, so their entire frame of reference is insurance. Furthermore, people who are licensed solely for insurance can sell you only this type of investment. Even if they thought other investments were more appropriate for you, they couldn't legally provide them to you. They may or may not even be aware of their inflexible bias, but they're going to find a way to convince you that insurance is the most appropriate investment for all your needs—and for the needs of everyone else they meet.

The Stockbroker

Next come securities sales: Your stockbroker handles these. If an adviser works on a commission basis and sells mutual funds, stocks, or insurance products that contain mutual funds, she must be licensed with the National Association of Securities Dealers (NASD).

Is it tough to get your securities license? Not at all. You simply get a brokerage firm to sponsor you. Then you complete an application, study for the exam, and pass it. This exam is a bit tougher than the insurance test—it takes two weekends to study for it, and the exam is about six hours long.

As easy as it is to obtain your securities license, the study materials and examination deal almost exclusively with regulatory issues—not with how to invest wisely for clients. In other words, a person passing the exam would be well schooled on keeping himself out of jail, but may not know anything about how to invest for you.

Depending on the test they take, salespeople can receive a license to sell only mutual funds (Series 6 license), mutual funds and individual stocks (Series 7 license), or to sell funds and stocks and also employ people to sell under their supervision (Series 24 license).

Please understand that an NASD-licensed salesperson could also have an insurance license. These people wear two hats, but everything they do is still based on a commission. When people are paid to sell, that's generally what they do. While exceptions exist, such individuals are usually not great at providing ongoing advice because they have no incentive to do so. *They make money only when you buy or sell something.* Sometimes the broker will call herself a financial adviser, but if she's working for you based on commissions, she's really a stockbroker or mutual fund seller.

Is your portfolio full of load mutual funds (A, B, or C shares)? If so, you probably get your advice from a licensed stockbroker who's really just a mutual fund seller. As explained in appendix D, A and B share mutual funds pay the salesperson a large up-front commission and small yearly fees. C share mutual funds pay the adviser 1 percent up front and up to 1 percent every year you hold the investment. As you have probably figured out, the mutual fund companies and the broker make their money as you buy and forget. That's why you rarely hear from these folks once they've made a sale. (Take note; if you have a greedy adviser, he'll sell you A or B shares and churn your account, frequently buying and selling. If you have a lazy adviser, he'll sell you C shares or a managed account and forget about you.)

Some stockbrokers have a different focus. Your statements might be full of individual stocks, which they buy and sell for you on a commission basis. If so, chances are your accounts are with a major stockbrokerage house. These people are Series 7–licensed and make money every time you buy and sell. Their focus is on *transactions*— not on growing your wealth.

Be cautious: few brokers are going to announce that they're commission brokers or mutual fund sellers. They may try to convince you that they're financial advisers. The only way you can know is if you ask them questions about their investment methodology and how they're compensated.

If they say they believe in asset allocation, buy and hold, always thinking long term, and having a long-term track record, these people simply want to hold your money without paying attention to the risks of the general market. If they tell you they're paid based on commissions, I also suggest you keep looking for a better fit.

The Registered Investment Adviser (RIA)

The alternative to commission-oriented advisers rests in fee based and hourly-based advisers. Yet finding someone who works on an hourly basis or for a fee rather than commission is no guarantee that she's in it for more than the quick buck. Those who charge fees must be registered either with the state or the Securities and Exchange Commission, depending on how big their practice is. But this registration is even easier than obtaining your securities or insurance license. It's simply a matter of taking an easy multiple-choice test, filling out a few forms, and sending in a check. The kid who got fired from the Quickie Oil Change place would have no problem passing this exam.

The Money Manager

A money manager is compensated to invest your money for you. Again, such people need to be registered as investment advisers because they'll charge a fee rather than earn commissions. In most cases, these people charge you a percentage of the assets they manage. For example, if you place $500,000 with them to manage, and they charge 1 percent, you'll pay $5,000 annually. (Aha! You're probably noticing that as your portfolio grows, so does the money manager's income from your account. This puts both of you on the same side of the table, working toward the same goal: increased wealth for you and your family. Yet you should also know that if your account declines, the money manager usually has a fee minimum, so he or she always gets paid, no matter what.) Money managers may also consult with you regarding retirement, tax, and estate planning. They might charge you additional fees or include those services if your account is large enough.

Many times, a financial planner is also a money manager. Sometimes your stockbroker will refer you to a money manager and split the fees with that person.

You might need a money manager, but keep in mind that not all money managers are alike. Again, you need to understand how this person manages money before you can determine whether or not the fit is good. Even though independent advisers have a greater incentive to protect and grow your assets, many don't develop the tools to do so. Fee-based advisers can be buy-and-forget-about-it bandits just as easily as other types.

Also keep in mind that if you're dealing with an adviser who's also a broker, you should not hold B or C shares in your accounts. If you did, you'd be paying the adviser twice for the same work. That's double dipping. Not kosher. Not prudent.

The Certified Financial Planner® (CFP®) Professional

The CFP designation indicates a certification, not a license. A stockbroker, insurance salesperson, financial planner, or money manager may also be a CFP professional, but nothing would necessarily change about the way they did business.

However, if your adviser has gone through the CFP certification, it does indicate a great deal of commitment to his profession. The process is rigorous and CFP certificants must agree "to adhere to the principles of integrity, objectivity, competence, fairness, confidentiality, professionalism, and diligence when dealing with clients."[1]

To become certified, you have to satisfy education, examination, experience, and ethics requirements. Some professionals, such as attorneys and CPAs, are exempt from the education requirement. But most people who end up with the CFP designation do satisfy all the requirements.

---

[1] Certified Financial Planner Board of Standards, Inc., Guide to CFP® Certification, www.cfp.net/become/certification.asp.

The education process takes roughly two years of intensive study. Applicants must pass an extensive exam covering seven topic areas: general financial planning, insurance planning, employee benefits, investment planning, income tax planning, retirement planning, and estate planning.

Once they take the examination successfully, they are eligible to apply for the CFP Certification Examination. This is an intense, two-day, 10-hour exam that assesses their ability to apply financial knowledge to real-life situations. Less than 60 percent of those who are eligible actually pass this examination. Those who do pass must satisfy the experience requirements, which vary according to whether or not they hold a college degree.

Finally, all CFP advisers have an ethics requirement. Once they successfully complete the education, examination, and experience requirements, they must complete a declaration stating whether or not they have ever been involved in any criminal, civil, governmental, or self-regulatory agency proceeding or inquiry. If they want the CFP certification, they must agree to adhere to the CFP Board's Code of Ethics.

The CFP certification demonstrates commitment and determination. It also gives the planner a good basis for providing clients with overall financial planning advice. However, it does not provide the planner with any expertise in managing money.

What It All Means

You can see that, regardless of the letters and numbers trailing after an adviser's name on his business card, the licensing and registration process has little to do with competence in terms of investing your money.

Commission brokers want to buy and sell for you. They aren't compensated to build wealth for you. People who sell you load mutual funds have a financial incentive to buy and forget about it.

Finally, fee-based advisers may have the incentive to protect you from bad markets, but they don't always have the tools to do it.

All of my comments are based on the concept that people do what they get paid to do. This is not to say that every commission-compensated salesperson is public enemy number one. Many of these people are sincerely interested in helping you as best they can. However, such individuals have the commission obstacle to overcome. Advisers may even come to believe they're working in the best interests of their clients, finding clever ways to justify their actions and fool even themselves. They might make recommendations to you with the best of intentions—but if they're compensated based on commissions, how can you ever be sure what their motivations really are?

Sometimes, the market says "stay away," but commission brokers and mutual fund sellers would go out of business if they gave you that advice. Instead, they find a way to believe that they shouldn't give such advice.

I find it amazing that in mid-2002, with the markets down as far as they were, advisers were *still* ignoring reality. I read a popular trade magazine for advisers, and one of the most well-respected writers in that journal continued hawking this buy-and-hold garbage. The article was teaching advisers how to explain to their clients that low prices are good and high prices are bad, that everything is on sale, and now's the time to load up on equities because over 30 years investing . . . yadda, yadda, yadda. By now you understand that they weren't listening to the market. Nope, they were listening to their dwindling bank accounts.

Headlines touted the "benefits" of staying invested in a volatile market (sure, there are benefits for the fund companies and brokers!) and lauded the "courage to underperform." Here's an actual headline guaranteed to steam your broccoli: "A Long-Term Correction Is Terrific for Investors!"

BE SELECTIVE • *Know How Advisers Work (You Over)*

What planet are these guys on? How could losing money be good for anyone? Heaven forbid these gurus consider the alternative: Maybe the markets are smarter than they are. Imagine that.

A Few Words about Brokers Who Sell IPOs

No discussion of the Wall Street money machine would be complete without covering initial public offerings, fondly referred to as IPOs. Even if you never invest in IPOs, it's important to understand how they work—and how brokers work for them. They mean big business, and that business influences the research your broker's firm provides to you.

Many large brokerage firms underwrite stocks. That means they help privately owned companies go public. Let's say an imaginary Acme Vacuum Cleaner Company is owned by Mrs. Simon. Mrs. Simon wants to expand the company, and to do so she needs capital (money). She goes to the equally fictitious Blarney Lunch stockbrokerage company for help. Together, they compromise on the value of the company. Let's say the company will be valued at $50 million and that Mrs. Simon needs $10 million to expand her business. Since $10 million is 20 percent of her company's value, she sells 20 percent of the business, and she issues 10 million shares valued at $1 per share. Mrs. Simon will hold onto 40 million shares—the remaining 80 percent.

The brokerage company can make many different kinds of deals with Mrs. Simon. For this example, Mrs. Simon tells Blarney Lunch that if they sell 10 million shares, they can keep everything they sell the shares for above $1. In other words, if the brokerage firm is able to sell the shares for $1.15 per share, they keep $0.15 for every share they sell—and Blarney Lunch makes a huge profit. This is why brokerage firms love IPOs.

This is what is known as underwriting or investment banking, and it's a big part of the profit that brokerage firms earn every year. Many big brokerage firms make much more profit in underwriting and investment banking than they do selling stocks to the public. In fact, many brokerage firms earn twice as much from IPOs as they do from retail commissions.

Once the firm agrees to bring the company public, how do they sell those shares? If the IPO is hot and the brokerage company expects great demand for the shares, the firm will allocate these hot shares to its best and largest clients. It can also use these hot IPO shares to reward and entice others to bring their investment banking business to the brokerage house.[2] Once these players get their shares, they'll hold onto them until the shares start trading publicly and sell for a tidy profit.

What about the IPOs of less attractive firms? This is where the stockbroker comes into play. It's important for you to understand that the firm's stockbrokers are often considered a distribution channel for these shares. That's the stockbroker's main function in many cases. The brokers may present themselves to the public as working on behalf of the investor, but the people who pay their salaries know otherwise.

The firm's stock analysts often publish glowing reports about how wonderful the company is so the broker has something to show you as the basis of his buy recommendation. (By the way, the analysts are not above reproach. In late April 2003, several were fined millions of dollars in answer to charges of deception, and the SEC voted unanimously to require all stock analysts to take an honesty vow and to vouch that the views expressed in research reports are actually their own. Gee, doesn't it reassure you to know

---

[2] As reported in the *New York Times*, *Wall Street Journal*, and *Investor's Business Daily* throughout 2003, many large brokerage firms, including Salomon Smith Barney, are being sued by several states for doling out hot IPO shares and favorable ratings to executives who steered their firms' investment banking business their way.

that they're taking vows now?) Regardless of the analysts' predictions, it doesn't matter much to the brokers if the companies they bring public are going to make you money or even survive; the brokerage house makes their money when you buy your shares. Need proof?

Of the 20 Internet companies that Merrill Lynch brought public since the start of 1997, 15 were trading below their offering prices and two had gone bust, as reported by *BusinessWeek*, April 16, 2001. Eight of those stocks had fallen 90 percent or more.[3] The greatest disaster was Pets.com, Inc., a company that went bust 10 months after its initial public offering.

Why do the brokerages bring shabby companies public? Call me crazy, but maybe, just maybe, it's the money. Big money. Henry Blodget helped make Merrill $100 million from 1997 through 2001. He explained why the firm brought so many companies public by saying that investors wanted these stocks. It would have been tough to tell a CEO he wouldn't take the company public when investors were shouting, "Bring it on!"[4]

In other words, Henry was trying to say that if Merrill hadn't done it, somebody else would have. I guess Henry was just following orders.

> *"Behavior is a mirror in which everyone shows his image."*
> JOHANN WOLFGANG VON GOETHE, Poet

---

[3] Peter Lestrom, "The Great Internet Money Game," *BusinessWeek* Online, April 16, 2001. http://www.businessweek.com/magazine/content/01_16/b3728602.htm

[4] Peter Lestrom, "The Great Internet Money Game."

Lush Profits—For the Brokerage House

If you were the stockbrokerage company, you'd want your brokers to sell those stocks that brought you the highest profit margin, right? Of course! And IPO profits are lush for Wall Street.

When your broker calls you up and offers you a "once in a lifetime opportunity to get in on the ground floor of Acme Vacuums," the real motivation might be for her firm to be more profitable. It might have nothing to do with what's in your best interest.

My advice is to stay away from IPOs and the brokers who sell them. The hot issues are probably not going to be available to the average investor. They'll be gobbled up by the large institutional investors and the broker's fat cat buddies first, leaving the average investor with the dregs that nobody else really wants. Of course, in the late 1990s when the market was in an all-time frenzy, even the worst IPOs were skyrocketing. But that was more a sign that the entire market was out of whack than a reflection of the value of those shares. In fact, the safest time to buy an IPO is three to six months after it's initially offered for sale.[5] What does this tell you? That IPOs are often overvalued when they're first offered for sale to the public.

Assume you made the mistake of buying an IPO: Why does your broker never suggest that you sell those shares? After all, when you sell, she rings up another commission. *(Cha-ching!)* She doesn't suggest it because of what would happen if you followed her advice: If your broker told you and every other client who held that stock to sell, and all those clients did sell their shares, the price of the stock would fall and reduce the value of the company. Make sense?

Think back to our example of Acme Vacuum Cleaner Company. The owner, Mrs. Simon, still owns 80 percent of the shares. Will she be happy if you and all the other stockholders dump your shares of

---

[5] William J. O'Neil, *How to Make Money in Stocks*, 3rd ed., 227.

Acme? The share price would plummet—and Mrs. Simon's net worth would disintegrate.

While the broker is not directly affected if the shares go down in value, it does affect the firm she works for—in a big way. Mrs. Simon paid the brokerage firm huge sums of money to bring the company public, and she wants the value of her shares to stay high so she can sell shares over time at good prices.

If the firm's brokers recommend that their clients sell, would Mrs. Simon ever come back to that firm for more business in the future? Nope. She'd go to another brokerage firm—one without pesky brokers who have the audacity to champion their clients' needs above their employers'.

Brokers know they might endanger the ability of their firm to attract new IPO business if they don't do their best to keep the share prices up—and they might jeopardize their jobs if they recommend you sell certain stocks. IPOs provide too much profit for Wall Street to have it any other way.

How to Find the Right Adviser

I don't think everyone needs a financial adviser. If you're the kind of person who likes to make your own investment decisions and you're comfortable with the results, why pay someone else to validate your thoughts?

Regardless of whether or not you use a financial adviser, it's important to read as many good books on the subject of investing as possible. I've included a few of my personal favorites in appendix A. This will help you ask better questions and make better decisions. However, books have their limitations. Books aren't dynamic; they don't take the market's temperature and advise you what to do on a daily basis.

More important, a book doesn't know you. A book doesn't know what's important to you about money, what you want to achieve, or what's important to you about life. This is why some people benefit by having a professional adviser.

If you do use an adviser, keep in mind that even the best have their limitations. Just because you pay someone for financial advice doesn't mean you have a right to expect perfection. Nobody can predict the future with certainty. So, with that caveat, how can you tell who's up to the task of earnestly helping you invest to reach your goals?

Look for Substance Over Style

Remember, almost anyone can claim to be a financial adviser. Keep in mind the varying degrees of licenses and certifications. My experience is that, as in any profession, the professional designations are much less important than the adviser's experience, motivations, investment methods, business goals, and communication skills.

Is the adviser aggressive and willing to do anything to reach high-income goals for himself? Or is the adviser interested in helping *you* achieve *your goals?* What's his focus? **Take note of the questions the financial adviser asks you. Pay attention to his communication skills. Don't undervalue your gut-level response to the person. Regardless of all else, if you don't feel comfortable with the adviser, move along.**

Here are some red flags: If they ignore risk, especially the risk of the overall market, stay away from them. (Can you remember the last time your broker suggested you move your money to a money market to avoid the carnage in the stock market? I didn't think you could.)

If a person provides *ongoing advice* on such areas as retirement planning, tax and estate planning, college funding, etc., he's probably a financial adviser. However, if a person talks about these issues superficially as a way to get in front of you to sell you something, he's probably just a stockbroker or insurance salesman. You'll know if you're talking to a person whose objective is only to sell something. No matter what he talks about in the beginning of the conversation, he'll get to why you have to invest in funds, insurance, or securities before the meeting is over.

Some hourly planners can, however, add real value when it comes to issues such as retirement or estate and college planning. They can provide you with the knowledge and understanding you need to make good decisions. But hourly planners really can't help you when it comes to investment management. That requires ongoing management, because the investment world is in a constant state of flux. For investment management, you need a money manager.

Bring Back That Lovin' Feeling

A financial planner should be someone you know (and who knows you) on a first-name basis. Many mutual fund companies try to convince the public that they can provide financial planning through toll-free phone numbers.

Well, if you rely on this type of financial advice, you'll never talk to the same person twice. This model doesn't create a relationship between you and the adviser. This might be a great way to sell you a fund, but it's not financial planning and it won't help you reach your goals.

The relationship between you and a financial planner is often as close as the relationship that you'd have with your pastor, doctor, or therapist. It's a personal relationship, and it can extend over many, many years.

Your adviser needs to understand you. To give you good advice, the adviser should care about you. Avoid firms that don't take a personal interest in you.

The Most Important Questions to Ask

It's critical to ask the adviser, "What's your investment strategy?" Does she have a risk management system? How does she protect your assets in declining markets?

You also need to ask how the adviser gets paid. If she charges you a fee, find out what those fees are. Are there any other fees? Do mutual fund companies or annuity companies pay her anything on top of what you pay her?

A-, B-, and C-class mutual funds are discussed in detail in appendix D. For now, just remember that if the broker sells you B or C shares, she can earn fees from the fund or annuity companies *on top* of the fees she charges you. This adviser is really a broker and clearly biased toward the fund or annuity company paying her a commission. Avoid this adviser like the plague.

How do you know if the fund or annuity you bought also pays your adviser any fees? Ask the adviser if you incur any penalty when you pull your money out of the investment—including within the first 12 months. If you do incur a penalty, the investment company is paying your adviser on top of what you're paying the adviser. Move along.

Beware of Trojan Horses

Obviously, referrals are important. Talk to your friends, colleagues, and relatives—anyone who you think makes good decisions about finances and can read a person's personality.

Many times, large institutions such as Schwab, Fidelity, or TD Waterhouse can refer you to an adviser. My personal experience is with TD Waterhouse and it's been excellent so far. The folks there take special care to match investors with the most appropriate advisers, and advisers don't provide TD Waterhouse with any financial incentives for sending them business. However, you must beware: In other firms, advisers pay thousands and thousands of dollars annually to be on a preferred provider list. Who gets that money? The institution that refers you to them!

Your main goal is to find the best adviser; their main goal is to auction you off to the highest bidder. Ask the adviser if he compensates the referring party in any way in exchange for the referral. And once you have that information, ask the referring party if they're compensated for referring or for putting advisers on a referral list. Let's keep everyone honest.

Talk to Your CPA

I'm impressed with most of the CPAs I've met. Most are genuinely concerned about their clients' well-being. Ask your accountant to recommend someone he or she feels comfortable with. But be careful—remember to ask even your CPA if there's any compensation for referring clients to the financial adviser. There's nothing wrong with CPAs and financial advisers working together; you simply want to understand the dynamics. Many CPAs set up arrangements with financial advisers to oversee their clients' investments. These CPAs spend time on the investments and should be compensated for their time. But your CPA must put your interests above the fee he collects for his oversight.

At the same time, be careful if your CPA wants to sell you investments directly or manage your money. How could he possibly have time to undertake both things well? I've been an investment adviser since 1984. I've been a Certified Financial Planner professional since 1996. It's a full-time job, and I don't have the time to prepare taxes for my clients on top of the work I already do. Likewise, an excellent CPA couldn't also be an excellent financial adviser. It just doesn't work. Want to test this out? Try calling your CPA in March and ask for investment advice—see what kind of response you get.

You Should Be Doing the Talking

Any adviser you talk with should ask you questions such as, "What's important about money to you?" "What are your goals?" "What do you want to achieve?" "What are some of the best investments or worst investments you've made?" "Have you worked with an adviser before?" "What was good about that person?" "What would you change if you could?"

In the initial interview, you should do most of the talking. If the adviser spends the time telling you how great he is, get out of there as soon as you can.

Check the regulators in your state to see if there's ever been a complaint against the adviser. In this instance, no news is good news.

Look for a Specialist

Ask the financial adviser what type of client she specializes in. Ask how many clients she has in each of the specialties. If you were a dentist and you interviewed a financial planner who deals only with dentists and surgeons, you'd probably feel comfortable that the adviser understands the unique challenges people in your position face. On the other hand, if you talked to a person who didn't specialize, you could find it difficult to communicate and feel understood.

Why You Want to Have an Assembly-Line Portfolio

This may sound counterintuitive, but you must insist on dealing only with an adviser who invests the same way for all of his clients.

I'll use my practice as an example. When I first entered my career, I told all my clients I would tailor their portfolios to meet their specific needs. That lasted for the first 10 clients. After that, I didn't have time to watch all the different stocks and mutual funds. Today, when I first meet new clients, I spend a great deal of time getting to know them and trying to understand what's important to them and what they value most.

I must admit that I'm rarely surprised by what I learn, because I focus my practice on three very clearly defined groups of people: retirees, highly paid employees, and small-business owners. I'm familiar with how these people think and what they want their money to do for them.

Let's say I meet a retiree who needs income, and we determine—given her age and income needs—that 60 percent of her assets should be invested in fixed income and 40 percent of her assets should provide equity growth.

For the 40 percent of her portfolio earmarked for growth, I use my safety net strategy. Not every client has 60 percent in fixed income and 40 percent in growth. Other clients' portfolios vary according to their specific needs, goals, and comfort level.

However, once we determine that a certain dollar amount should be invested for growth, I use the exact same strategy and exact same investments for all clients investing for growth. I use the same or similar bonds or preferred shares for the income portion of the portfolio for all clients who want income.

You may be wondering how I could possibly do this. What if a client wanted to be more aggressive? Remember, I deal with only three distinct types of people. These are people I understand, and typically these people don't want to be super-aggressive. Hence, my method is appropriate for the people I want to serve. If a client wants to be more aggressive than my model provides, I don't accept the client because we aren't a good match.

How does this type of streamlined money management help clients? A uniform approach is much easier for the adviser: Since she doesn't spend hours and hours poring over 200 individual portfolios, she can spend that time making sure your needs are being met, doing research to keep on top of the market, and tracking those few investments she does hold.

By working with an adviser who implements her investment method with all of her clients, you'll have an efficient adviser who'll have the time to do what you're paying her to do—manage your money without taking undue risk so you can do the things that are most important to you. So please look for an adviser who uses an investment process that fits your needs and comfort level.

Don't Judge a Book by Its (Expensive) Cover

Watch out for advisers who try to sell you expensive financial plans. I'm not a big fan of the typical financial plans that many advisers produce for clients, which are about three inches thick and show lots of colored charts and graphs. They look very good and cost an arm and a leg, but they don't create much value—they're often so complicated that clients simply ignore them.

More important, such a financial plan projects your future based on your situation today. The plan assumes that nothing is going to change. But everything changes. Your financial situation, the economy, interest rates, inflation, your family situation, and your goals are all subject to change.

Of course, it's important to plan for the future, but I favor an interactive and dynamic financial-planning process. Such a plan should require four to five hours of the planner's time (for most client situations) and should be priced accordingly. Unless your situation is extremely complicated, be wary of someone who wants to sell you a plan that requires more than four to five hours of his time.

Points of Interest

▸ Know what you want before you visit with a financial planner. Are you interested in money management or general finances such as insurance, estate planning, college-tuition financing, etc.?

▸ Talk to other people whom you trust and who are in a similar situation. If you're retired, talk to other retirees. If you're a small-business owner, talk to other small-business owners.

▸ In the case of a Registered Investment Adviser (those advisers who work on a fee or hourly basis), ask for a registration or disclosure statement. This is known as the Form ADV Part II, and it details the planner's conflicts of interest, business background, and qualifications. It also explains how the planner is compensated. Ask to see the planner's contracts, and be sure to understand exactly what you should expect to receive in exchange for the fees you'll be paying.

▸ Make sure you feel at ease with the planner. You should be comfortable asking questions. If your planner makes you feel uncomfortable after you ask questions, move on the next planner. The relationship between planner and client should be for the long term. Make sure you get your money's worth and understand that this is a two-way street. Both parties should benefit. Neither of you are doing the other a favor; this is serious business—this is your life. You shouldn't work with a planner who gives you the feeling he's doing you a favor by working with you. Also, if you feel you're doing a favor to the adviser by working with him, move on.

▸ Make sure the planner has well-defined investment strategies that she uses for all her clients. The planner should be able to explain how buying and selling decisions are made. The planner should have a well-defined method of reducing the risk to which her clients are exposed.

- Interview more than one planner: Ask each of them to detail their educational background, professional experience, and specialties or niches served. Ask about the size of the practice and how long they've been in business. How do they communicate with clients and how often? How big is their staff? (If the planner also answers all the calls and mail, handles client service, etc., she probably doesn't have the time to do what you want her to do—manage your financial assets.) Ideally, look for a planner with at least one full-time assistant.
- Ask the adviser for a complete list of the licenses and certifications she holds. Then, ask the adviser how you can check up on her status with each of these organizations. You should be interested in how the adviser reacts. If she quickly provides you with a list and tells you how to contact each organization, she probably has nothing to hide. I still suggest you contact each organization and ask whether or not the adviser has any complaints registered against her or an adverse regulatory history.[6] You never know what you'll find. If the adviser hems and haws about providing you the information, I suggest you find another adviser pronto.
- IPOs are great money-makers for brokerage houses, not for you.
- Brokers are used by their employers to sell IPOs because they create such huge profits.
- Many IPOs are priced lower three to six months after their initial offering.
- Brokers have an incentive to advise you to hold the shares you bought as an IPO—they never want you to sell.
- Most investors should stay away from IPOs and not believe Wall Street research.

---

[6] Go to www.NealFrankle.com for information on how to contact these organizations.

- Bottom line: You must feel comfortable with your adviser, and you must understand how the adviser manages money. You must feel that the person is trustworthy and that this person has your interests at heart. Don't settle for second best. Keep searching until you feel comfortable.

Exercises

1. Swear an oath on a Holy Bible or other sacred religious text that you'll never invest in IPOs.
2. Call your financial adviser(s) and ask what licenses and certifications they have.
3. Ask them how they get paid, if you don't already know.
4. Ask how your money is being managed and how the adviser protects you in bad markets.

Get Real
Recognize Asset Allocation for What It Truly Is (And Is Not)

"Repetition does not transform a lie into a truth."
FRANKLIN D. ROOSEVELT, 32nd U.S. President

Asset allocation has become a watchword among many financial advisers because it just sounds so good when they present the strategy to investors. It's a method of diversification, or keeping all your eggs out of one basket. The theory is that by spreading your money around, you reduce risk and volatility in your portfolio. When one asset class goes down, another class goes up, and by not having all your money in one place, you avoid catastrophic losses.

Sound good so far?

You invest a portion of your money in stocks, in bonds, and in real estate and you stay invested 100 percent of the time. Using asset allocation, the portion in stocks is split into different pools of money. One pool is invested in large-cap value, another in large-cap growth, and still others in mid-cap value, mid-cap growth, international, emerging growth, etc.

Of the money invested in bonds, you would own short-term bonds, intermediate-term bonds, long-term bonds, corporate bonds, government bonds, etc. In short, you'd have money invested in a variety of areas within each category or asset class.

In theory, this sounds wonderful. An investor relying on asset allocation would forget about the general health of the market and dismiss specific areas of strength or weakness within the market. Asset allocators simply spread their money over several asset classes and hold on.

Great, right? Are you ready to sign up?

Don't get your pen out yet; there are some serious flaws in the asset-allocation strategy promoted by most financial advisers, not the least of which is a major crack in the foundation on which it's built.

A Faulty Foundation

In 1986, a study was done by the noted economists Brinson, Hood, and Beebower.[1] They claimed that asset allocation was responsible for 93.6 percent of the variability in an investor's return. In other words, Brinson and friends found that the *fluctuation* of the return in a portfolio is caused by how the assets are allocated. For example, a portfolio made up of stocks might go up and down more than a portfolio of bonds. That's clear enough. The study did not try to predict or evaluate the actual return (the gain or loss) of the portfolio.

Many "professionals" in the financial services industry took that conclusion and ran with it. Along the way, they either misunderstood or knowingly misinterpreted the study. With its presentation, they convinced investors that if they diversified their money in a certain way, they could hold onto that allocation, forget about the market, and count on earning a great return. Sound familiar? The fund industry benefits because this boosts investor confidence in the buy-and-forget-about-it model. What a windfall for the financial services industry![2]

Make no mistake: Asset allocation is just a sophisticated buy-and-forget-about-it ploy. Brokers show you other wonderful charts and hope you fall for it. They have, so why wouldn't you?

---

[1] Gary P. Brinson, L. Randolph Hood, and Gilbert L. Beebower, "Determinants of Portfolio Performance," *Financial Analysts Journal* 42 (July/August 1986), 39–44.

[2] Roger G. Ibbotson, "The True Impact of Asset Allocation on Returns" reported that a 1998 survey by Nuttall & Nuttall showed that only 2 percent of those writers surveyed correctly quoted the Brinson study.

Does Asset Allocation Work?

Even though some in the investment world tout asset allocation as the cure-all to investor woes, many financial experts call asset allocation a hoax. William Jahnke, chairman and chief investment officer of Financial Design Educational Corporation and recipient of the 1974 Graham & Dodd Award of excellence given by the Association for Investment Management and Research®, said, "The idea that a static strategic asset allocation policy [buy and forget about it] makes no economic sense does not appear to present a problem for investment advisers who advocate [buy and forget about it] fixed-weight asset allocations. However, the unfortunate result for many investors . . . will be the failure of their asset allocation and saving program to achieve their financial goals."[3]

Interpreted, Dr. Jahnke calls asset allocation a lot of, well, noise. Aldo Svaldi explains his findings this way:

> Jahnke poses several troubling questions, however. The 1986 study also found that over a 10-year time frame, the mix of assets only explained 14.6 percent of the range of a portfolio's returns. The specific investments picked and the timing of those picks do matter as far as overall return over a longer time horizon.
>
> Taking a pill that is 94 percent effective is much different than taking one 14.6 percent effective. The problem is that most investors believe they are swallowing the first [when they invest using asset allocation] and are told as much, when the second is what they are getting, Jahnke said.[4]

---

[3] William W. Jahnke, "The Asset Allocation Hoax," *Journal of Financial Planning*, February 1997.

[4] Aldo Svaldi, "Are You Being Served by Asset Allocation?" *Denver Business Journal*, March 24, 1997.

A popular source of stock analysis, Morningstar found that how much you earn on your investments is due to the following factors:[5]

1. Selection, 38 percent
2. Aggressiveness, 28.1 percent
3. Style timing, 27.2 percent
4. Asset allocation, 16.5 percent
5. Market timing, 3.9 percent
6. Style, 2.9 percent

Hmmm. Asset allocation didn't make the top of the list. Or even the top three. Here, it's number four with an unimpressive 16.5 percent. But didn't Jahnke say 14.6 percent and your broker (citing the Brinson team) report 93.6 percent? Why didn't Morningstar confirm one of those figures? First, as I pointed out earlier, the original Brinson study found that the *variability or fluctuation* of returns (and not the return itself, as the fund industry misreported) is explained by asset allocation. Morningstar was evaluating actual earnings. Second, the Morningstar study covered a specific 10-year period, which in this case was when the markets were rising. In a different 10-year period, the results could be very different. Certainly, in the bad market we experienced from 2000 through 2002, aggressive funds did worse than the general market. This would probably mean aggressiveness was most important in determining (poor) performance.

From 1987 through 1996, the best way to maximize your return would have been aggressiveness. In different time periods, different factors become much more important. I guess things do change after all. Too bad the classic model of asset allocation fails to recognize this.

---

[5] Susan Paluch, "When Good Research Turns Bad," *Morningstar Investor* 6 (September, 1997).

Why Asset Allocation Doesn't Work

The basic idea of asset allocation is that if one asset class falls, another goes up to compensate. This may be true at some points in time, but it isn't always true. Generally, asset allocation doesn't make sense because most stocks move *with* the overall market and because it's just dumb to arbitrarily hold lame investments.

A study released in 2003 by investment giant T. Rowe Price compared four differently allocated portfolios to one U.S. stock fund. If you'd invested $10,000 per year in each of these portfolios for the past 20 years, even after the gut-wrenching period of 2000–2002, you'd have significantly more money had you bypassed asset allocation and stuck with the stock fund made up 100 percent of a variety of domestic stocks: no bonds, no foreign stocks.[6]

Why? Because each of the allocation portfolios held low-performing assets over many years. Even the so-called "aggressive" asset allocation portfolio put 10 percent in boring bonds and 15 percent in flaccid foreign stocks. As a result of being weighted down with these underperforming investments, all of the asset-allocated portfolios did poorly. The stock fund beat all the allocated funds because it was invested only in stocks over that 20-year period.[7]

---

[6] Paul Katzeff, "Asset Allocation Strategies Have Limits," *Investor's Business Daily*, 11/24/03.
[7] Paul Katzeff, "Asset Allocation Strategies Have Limits."

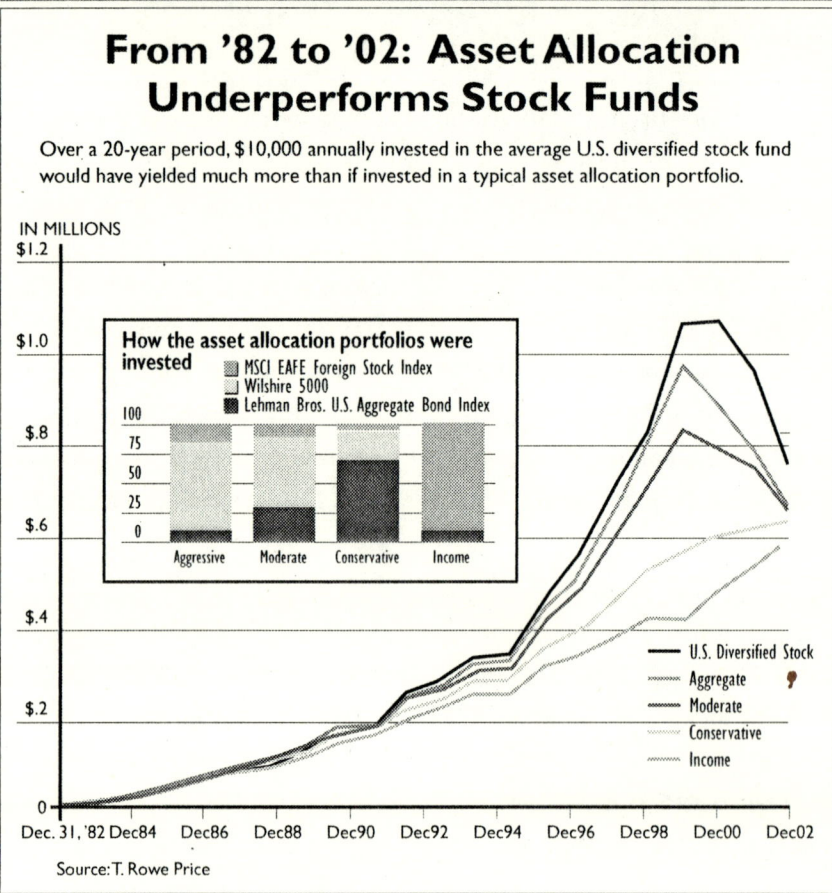

Another problem is the asset allocation model is rather static. It calls for you to have set percentages of your assets in the various asset classes. These set percentages don't change much. Sure, you have a bit of rebalancing, but for the most part, it's "Damn the torpedoes, full speed ahead!" Well, damn the torpedoes with someone else's money, not with yours.

Why Advisers Love Asset Allocation

Many financial advisers, stockbrokers, and financial service providers continue to recommend the asset allocation strategy because they know of no other alternative to manage money—and because they continue to misunderstand the Brinson report. Of course, they say they recommend it to protect their clients' assets.

But the clearest reason for their recommendation, in my opinion, is that as long as you stay diversified and hold those investments, you continue paying fees on an ongoing basis. As a result, asset allocation allows the stockbroker to be out playing golf, going on long vacations, and driving Jaguars. As long as he can convince you to *hold no matter what*, his calendar stays clear.

My sense is that asset allocation is one of those fancy ideas your broker has that just doesn't sit well with you, either. After all, the world changes constantly. Shouldn't your investments change to protect you in bad markets and take advantage of opportunities as they present themselves?

> *"Courage is a special kind of knowledge:
> the knowledge of how to fear
> what ought to be feared and
> how not to fear what ought not to be feared."*
> DAVID BEN-GURION, Soldier and Statesman

Asset Allocation: The Real Deal

Here's a more useful application of asset allocation, one that relates directly to your values and goals. First, forget this nonsense about holding onto equal-weighted asset classes. We've exposed what a fairy tale that is. Instead, think about your goals and when you want to achieve them. Once you're clear on those two variables, allocate your money into the most appropriate investments to reduce risk.

For example, if you have a certain amount of money, and your goal is to fund your 15-year-old daughter's college expenses, you have no business investing everything in equities. You'll need at least part of that money in three years.

If you have three- to five-year goals, you should keep the cash allocated to those goals in money markets, short-term bonds, CDs, or treasury bills. At the end of the term, your money will be there and you'll be able to send your daughter off to school. These short-term investments offer zero risk: they don't endanger or jeopardize the attainment of your goal. The percentage profit return isn't that important when you consider short-term goals; liquidity and safety are much more important.

Conversely, if you're 55 years old and you want to invest for your retirement, ask yourself, "Since I'm going to retire in 10 years and stay retired for 20 years, what's the best way to invest over that time horizon?" In such a situation, a conservative equity portfolio would probably make the most sense.

Let's look at some numbers. Assume you have $50,000 earmarked for a college fund that you'll need in five years. (In other words, for five years, you can invest the money and not touch it, but at the end of the five years you'll spend all of the money.)

You have two investment choices: You can either invest the money at 5 percent and take no risk, or you can invest the money at 8 percent and take some risk. Assume further that if you don't have at least the $50,000 at the end of five years, you won't be able to achieve your financial goal: your daughter won't attend college.

If you invest the money for five years at 5 percent, it will grow to $63,800 by the end of the term. You've reached your goal and you'll have a few extra dollars to spare.

GET REAL • *Recognize Asset Allocation for What It Truly Is (And Is Not)*

Now, if you're able to grow the money at 8 percent, you'll have $73,000 at the end of the five-year period. In other words, you'll have almost $10,000 more than with the 5 percent investment alternative if everything goes right.

The problem with the 8 percent investment is that in order to achieve the potential higher return, you have to take risk. Things could go wrong. In fact, you might have a negative 5 percent return (or worse) for the entire period. If that were the case, you wouldn't have the $50,000 that you need. If you lost 5 percent per year, your capital would be $39,000 at the end of five years. And that could happen.

If it does happen, you won't achieve your goal. Your child won't go to college. She'll stay home with you and your spouse—for the next 40 years.

Do you really want your spouse and daughter whining, "I told you not to make those investments!" for the next 40 years?

Does it make sense to take the risk of not sending your child to college for the potential gain of $10,000? The extra $10,000 won't change your life. Your daughter not going to college *will* affect your life—and hers.

In this case, a proper way to allocate your investments would be to buy secure investments that are guaranteed, with the entire $50,000.

On the other hand, let's look at your retirement accounts.

Assume you're 55 years of age and you have retirement accounts worth $150,000. Further assume that you'll retire at age 65 in 10 years, and that you're going to stay retired for 20 years. In other words, you plan to live to 85, another 30 years from now.

Let's examine how your investment decision impacts your income.

Let's assume, again, that you're 55 years old and you have $150,000 invested in a retirement plan. You invest this money for 10 years, and in the tenth year you start taking withdrawals. Assume that over the next 20 years, the money continues to grow at the same rate it did over the prior 10 years. Starting in the 10th year, your yearly withdrawal will be just enough so that at the end of 20 years, you will have exhausted the entire portfolio.

You have two investment alternatives; how does each affect your capital and income over the life of the investment plan (30 years)?

In alternative one, you invest $150,000 for 10 years and it grows at 5 percent annually. At the end of 10 years you have $244,000. Assuming the account continues to grow at 5 percent every year, you can withdraw a little over $19,000 every year for 20 years before you run out of money.

In the second alternative, you invest the $150,000 at 8 percent and accept greater short-term risk. You grow the money for 10 years, at which time it would be worth $324,000. Very nice. But that isn't the important part. Assuming the portfolio continues to earn 8 percent over the 20-year withdrawal period, the real impact is that your income would be almost $33,000 a year.

Did you get that? Your income almost doubles. Nicer vacations. Better health care. More freedom, more flexibility, less stress. The brass ring. You got it all.

As pretty as this picture seems, the big problem with using equity to achieve long-term goals is short-term volatility. (You see in this chapter that you should allocate long-term investments to equity. You see in previous chapters that you can't buy and forget about your equity investments. Tools to reconcile this conflict are in chapter 7.)

However, these two simple examples (college and retirement funding) illustrate a better application of asset allocation. **Match your investments with your time horizon.** As you can see, equity investments are far more powerful when it comes to the retirement goals because (in this example) you have more time. Because of the greater time period, the higher return potential in equity

GET REAL • Recognize Asset Allocation for What It Truly Is (And Is Not)

compounds longer. Also, because of the long time frame, the risks are lower. The impact of any one (negative) year is significantly reduced. This type of asset allocation makes a lot of sense to me.

What *doesn't* make sense is to blindly plunk your money into investments that are underperforming and watch your assets disappear—just what classic asset allocation suggests you do. **Use asset allocation to help you decide how best to achieve your short-term, intermediate-term, and long-term goals by providing broad guidelines for investing.** As your time frame and capital base become greater, tap into the power of equity investing. But please have a method to reduce risk. If you have less time and capital, rely on the safety of money markets and debt instruments. That's all the asset allocation you need to understand.

Consider All Your Goals

If you think you have only long-term goals, you're mistaken. Almost everyone has short-term, mid-term, and long-term financial needs. Take the example of a newly retired couple. Their short-term needs are for daily living expenses and emergency loans to their children. Their mid-term needs include replacing their 1974 Pontiac in two years. Their long-term needs include retirement income. It's critically important for this couple to use different investments to achieve each of these different goals.

If they make the mistake of placing all their assets in equity, they take undue risk. What would they do if a short-term emergency came up? They'd be forced to invade their equity investments. They may have to sell off some of their long-term investments at a bad time.

When people do this, they jeopardize their short-term, mid-term, and long-term financial goals. That's why it's critically important for you to first identify all your financial goals, then determine the time horizon for each goal. Last, invest in a consistent manner to achieve your goals.

When you make an investment, think of your goal as the defining factor. Is this money for your next house? When are you planning on buying it? Is it for college or retirement? When do you need the money and for how many years? Is it for your next vacation in Maui? When are you leaving? Group your goals into common time frames, then invest your money according to those needs.

Points of Interest

- The classic model of asset allocation includes having a percentage of your money invested in a variety of different asset classes. This model does not consider the current market conditions or risk. The theory is that while one asset class goes down, others rise, which theoretically reduces risk.
- This model exposes clients to great risk because when one market declines, other markets can decline as well.
- If your adviser suggests an asset allocation model to manage your assets, ask her to prove how it will help you achieve your life goals. She won't be able to.
- You're better served by allocating long-term investments to achieve long-term goals, mid-term investments to mid-term goals, and short-term investments to short-term goals.
- As your time frame increases, consider equity investments.
- If you want to safeguard your long- and mid-term assets, make sure you have enough short-term investments available. This way, when an emergency comes up, you won't have to invade your long- and mid-term investments to meet short-term emergencies.

GET REAL • *Recognize Asset Allocation for What It Truly Is (And Is Not)*

Exercises

1. List five goals that are very important to you and your family. List the exact date and the exact amount of money you need or want to achieve these goals.
2. How many years from today will it be before you need each sum of money?
3. Given that, what's the best way to invest now to achieve each of those goals?

Choose Carefully
Buck the Wall Street System: Select Investments That Are Right for You

"A serious person does not wait for the words of the critic; he checks himself. Deep in his heart, he knows what his standards should be, and he strives to be faithful to them."
MARIAN ANDERSON, Opera Singer

Some investors are convinced that funds are for suckers and individual stocks are better (or vice versa). Other investors simply don't know which way to go. To determine whether funds or stocks are right for you, you have to go back to your goals and values. What are you trying to achieve? What's important to you about money? If your ultimate goal is to have less stress, more fun, more flexibility, and no worries about your money, then fund investing is probably suitable for you.

If you own individual stocks, you could strike gold overnight, but with funds that probably won't happen.

Of course, it would be nice to strike gold, but is it worth the risk you take? For most people who simply want to grow their assets while enjoying adequate income, funds probably do the best job of helping you control risk and achieve your goals.

Please don't misunderstand me. You *can* use individual stocks to create wealth. I use individual stocks, but only for those clients who are comfortable with taking added risk. Also, and this is very important, I suggest that you use individual stocks if, and only if, the market has really proven itself to be strong.

The general health of the market is responsible for most of the return on your investments,[1] and this is certainly true with mutual

---
[1] William J. O'Neil, *How to Make Money in Stocks*, 3rd ed.

funds. For most investors, simply capturing the good returns of a healthy market and avoiding the catastrophic losses of a poor market yield enough to help achieve financial goals. If you can accomplish that, why take the added risk of owning individual stocks?

Consider the numerous times an investor goes to sleep at night with her stock at $40 per share, only to wake up the next morning and discover that the price fell to $25. Why does this happen? Maybe the SEC discovers what the president of the company has been up to. Maybe the company's accounting department is the target of a government audit. Because of problems like these, your stock could tank even in a great market—but that's nothing compared to what could happen to such a stock in a poor market environment.

By way of example, look at what happened to Tenet Healthcare, a stock market darling. Tenet suffered a 70 percent loss over a two-week period. Now, that's enough to ruin anyone's weekend!

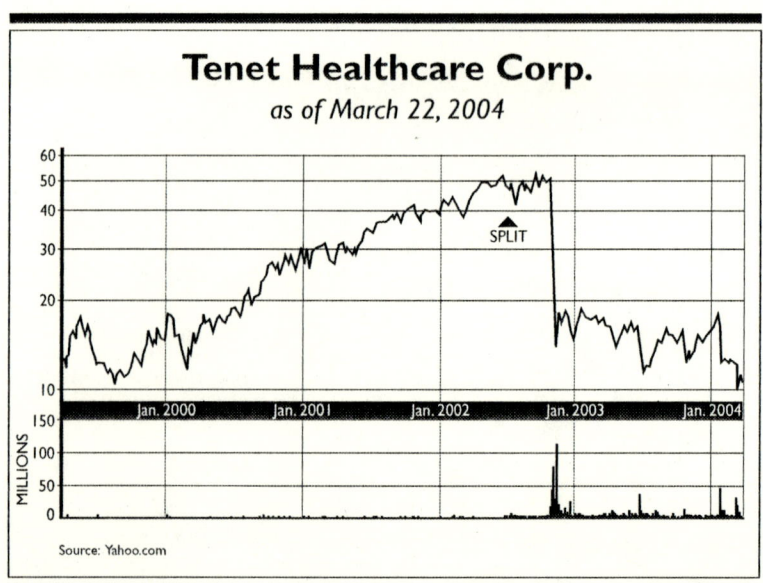

In a bad market environment, investors are ultrasensitive to any bad news, and your stock may get clobbered as investors dump it fast. Things can happen quickly. With an individual stock, you may not have enough time to react to safeguard your assets. Funds can give you more time.

Generally, funds allow you that breathing space because they're often made up of hundreds of different stocks. It's unlikely that any one stock will make up more than 1 to 2 percent of your fund portfolio. If you own a stock within a fund, and that stock does poorly, it's unlikely to affect your account values significantly since it makes up such a small percentage of your overall account.

Given this, why do some investors insist on owning individual stocks? Some people argue that direct stock investors have full control over their portfolios and their taxes. They can decide when to buy and sell, rather than being forced to rely on some highfalutin' fund manager. (Their arguments don't bother to mention that most individual investors haven't got the slightest idea as to what to buy, when to buy it, or when to sell it.)

Individual stock investors crow that they have no fund management fees to pay. They criticize mutual funds, saying they can't match the performance of the broader stock market, despite the expertise of the fund managers. Another complaint is that funds are not tax efficient: An owner of a fund could actually see the value of the fund decline one year and yet still receive a tax bill at the end of the year.

Big Benefits of Mutual Funds (and How to Minimize Any Potential Drawbacks)

Given all the drawbacks mentioned above, why would anyone want to buy mutual funds?

Allow me to examine each of these issues.

Expenses

Some funds do have high expenses but not all. Clearly, I would look for those funds with the least management expense and the best amount of return for the least amount of risk. Index funds and exchange-traded funds (ETFs) sometimes offer just that.[2]

Fund expenses can range—exclusive of loads—from 0.2 percent to 3 percent annually. The average expense is 1.55 percent.[3] If you stick with the lower expense funds, then cost should not be a major obstacle. Since funds report returns net of fees, you can also compare the low-cost to average or even high-cost funds in terms of performance before you invest.

I admit that if you buy and sell stocks yourself, you avoid paying fund management fees. But is the money you save by managing the money yourself worth the emotional anguish, time spent, and potential losses you face as a result? When you buy individual stocks, you have to keep your eye on many variables. In most cases, it's not worth it. If you currently manage your own stocks, all you have to do is ask yourself, "How's this going so far? Am I pleased with my results?" If you were, I doubt you'd be reading this book.

Some folks ask brokers to manage a portfolio of stocks for them. What does that cost? It's not uncommon to find their fees exceeding 2.5 percent per year—much higher than most mutual fund fees!

---

[2] www.iShares.com lists the expense ratios of each of their iShares. Their Russell indexes range in expense from .15 to .25. In contrast, the average mutual fund expense is approximately 1.5. This is six times as expensive as the Russell index iShares.

[3] *Facts About Mutual Funds,* Investment Company Institutute: 1999.

There are many other problems inherent in having brokers manage your stocks for you, and we examined the real cost of that in chapter 5.

Control

Stock investors complain that when you own a fund, you never know what the fund is doing. What is the manager buying and selling? What companies does the fund own at any one time? These investors explain that by having their broker buy individual stocks, they maintain control because they always know what stocks are being held in their accounts.

Well, this is true. But it doesn't matter—it's just plain irrelevant.

If you want to get a haircut, you shouldn't care if the barber uses clippers or scissors. If you trust the barber and feel comfortable that he understands your needs and has your best interests at heart, what do you care how he gets it done, as long as he gets the job done, and done well?

If you're flying from Los Angeles to New York, do you ask what type of jet fuel is being used? Of course not. All you care about is arriving safely and on time.

My wife and I wanted to purchase a new car recently. (Please understand that I know nothing about cars!) We visited a dealership, and when we got to the showroom, the salesperson popped the hood on the car we were interested in and showed me the engine. I couldn't have cared less. I didn't even know what I was looking at. I'd done my research on safety and reliability before I arrived in the showroom. All I was concerned about once I got there was the smoothness of the ride and the price. Is this making sense?

Do you need to look under the hood of your investments? Why? If you do, will anything make sense to you? Probably not—it's far better to do your research on the investment method and stick to it. You need to have a great method by which to evaluate what funds or stocks you buy and when to buy. Then leave the driving to the investment method.

When it comes to money, all you should really care about is growing your money safely so you can enjoy more and worry less—right? That's the destination you planned. Control is much more important when it comes to *how* you invest, rather than *what* individual fund or stocks you invest in. The investment method you use will have a much greater impact on your results than a specific fund or stock decision will.

Besides, if you thought you knew how to manage money better than a fund manager, you'd probably open your own mutual fund. If your ultimate goal is to worry less about your money and have more time to spend on the really important things in life, why would you even waste a moment of your time worrying about which stocks are bought and sold on your behalf? If you have a great investment method that's consistent with your needs and personality, this micromanagement control issue disappears.

Performance

When stock buyers think about performance, they're thinking of potential gains. I agree that individual stock investors could do substantially better than fund investors if the stocks they owned took off. But in a bad market, the individual stock investor could get wiped out. Game over: insert quarter. If you have one left.

I find that people get significantly more attached to their individual stocks than they do to mutual funds. "This stock has been so good to me . . . I just can't sell it!" "I ride Harley Davidson bikes, so how can you ask me to sell their stock? I love that company!" "I've worked for WorldCom all my life and the company was good to me . . . I've built a great retirement; how can you ask me to sell the stock now?"

Folks get emotionally attached to stocks and find it harder to sell when they should. They hold onto stocks longer and lose more money than they have to because of that emotional attachment. I call *this* lack of control. You can see that this lack of control can cost an investor big bucks, and ultimately destroy a portfolio's performance.

On the other hand, few investors become emotionally attached to mutual funds—this lack of emotional attachment is a huge benefit!

Taxes

Investors sometimes feel they should never buy funds because they think that they must pay taxes on "gains" even if the fund loses money. This can happen, but it's optional for the most part. If you have a taxable account and you sell an individual stock at a gain, you're liable for income tax. If a stock is worth more than you paid for it, but you don't sell the stock, you don't owe any tax.

When you own mutual funds, even if you don't sell, you may have to pay taxes every year. It doesn't even matter if the shares of the fund go up or down. Why?

The mutual fund manager buys and sells stocks during the year. If this results in a net profit, the manager creates a capital gain. The capital gain is passed on to you—and you're responsible for the taxes. This is true whether you reinvest the capital gain or receive the capital gain as cash, and can be a real pain. It's one negative to owning funds. But in reality, this tax is mostly voluntary. If you don't want to pay that tax, you usually don't have to. How is this possible? By a method that I love to use for my clients, called tax loss harvesting.

Let's say you own the ABC fund. You bought it for $100 in January of this year and by December it's priced at $90 per share. The market was poor. So your shares decrease in value and on top of that, the fund pays out a $20 capital gain on which you have to pay taxes.

Why do they pay out a capital gain if the value of the shares in the fund decreases? Because during the year, that fund buys and sells stocks. If the market is in turmoil, many times people take their money out of the funds. For the fund manager to give these investors their money, she must sell some of her holdings. The manager may sell holdings at a profit. These profits generate the capital gains.

This is very common. For our example, assume the fund manager buys and sells during the year, and the average gain is $20 per share in the fund.

This means that you as a shareholder of the fund are stuck with a tax bill on the $20 capital gain, even though you didn't sell your shares and even though the shares have decreased in value. If you were in the 20 percent tax bracket (capital gains), you'd owe $4 in tax (per share) unless you did something about it.

Here are a few things you could do to take a big bite out of that tax bill.

STEP 1: Keep in mind that the day the fund pays out the gain, the value of the fund decreases by roughly the same amount. In our example, all things being equal, if the shares are worth $90 the day before the gain is paid, and $20 is paid out, the fund value drops to $70 on the day that the gain is paid out. Why?

Because that $20 the manager paid out comes from somewhere—from the value of the fund.

Imagine you're back in third-grade math class and the teacher asks what happens if you have five apples and you give two of them to your friend Billy. How many apples do you have left? Three! Right you are. Apples and funds, the math works the same. If you have a fund worth $90 and the fund pays out $20, what do you have left? Again, right you are: $70.

Now what can you do with that $20 capital gain? You can either spend it or reinvest it in the fund. If you reinvest it, you receive $20 worth of additional shares in the ABC Fund. *In this particular case, you'd receive 2/7 of one additional share ($20/$70).* If you add up the value of your *original* share ($70) plus the capital gain ($20) reinvested in 2/7 of a share, what do you have? If you said $90, you are right.

If you do nothing at this point, you have a share and reinvested dividends worth $90 (which is less than you paid in January)—*and* you have to pay a capital gains tax on the distribution. The tax will cost you $4.

STEP TWO: **To wipe out the tax that was created by the capital gain, sell all your shares on the day after the capital gains are paid out.** Put the proceeds into another similar fund with a similar strategy. By reinvesting immediately in a similar fund, you don't have to worry about being out of the market at the wrong time, and you don't have to worry about paying the capital gains tax.

What have you accomplished by doing this?

Well, you have a $20 gain because the ABC mutual fund paid out a $20 capital gain. But since you bought the ABC Fund at $100 in January and you sold it for $70 in December, you recognize a $30 capital loss. This offsets the $20 gain, and, therefore, you don't have to pay any tax. You actually create a tax loss, which you can use against other gains this year or in the future. Isn't this marvelous?

The bottom line is, there are many strategies you can use to reduce the impact of capital gains distributions from your mutual funds. Even though you can't do anything about the amount these funds pay out in dividends, you certainly can do a lot about how much of it you pay taxes on.

Also, as a general rule, you should look for funds that historically don't have huge capital gains payouts. One way to do this is by searching for funds with low turnover. Turnover is just jargon for the number of times the fund manager buys and sells the stocks that make up the portfolio. The greater the turnover rate, the more the manager buys and sells stocks. This means there's a greater likelihood that the manager realizes more gains and losses during the year and thus creates a higher tax bill for you. Higher turnover usually also means higher expenses, since it costs money to buy and sell stocks—even for funds.[4] The more they buy and sell stocks, the higher the turnover, and the higher the cost to you. You can determine what your fund's turnover rate is by reviewing a Morningstar report or calling the fund.

The bottom line is that taxes don't have to affect you if you own mutual funds. It's mostly a matter of choice. From now on, just say no to taxes on your capital gains from mutual funds!

You now see how the tax problem is certainly manageable. But in case you still have a few lingering doubts, let me make one final comment on taxes in the form of a question.

Wouldn't you love to have paid $1 million in capital gains tax on gains you made in the stock market in 2001 and 2002?

Sure you would. Do you know anyone who held onto certain stocks "because they couldn't afford to pay the tax on the gain," only to see those gains melt quickly into losses? If you're like me, you know too many people who've suffered from this problem.

I'm sure you agree that it's much better to pay taxes on gains than to have losses and not pay taxes.

The tax issue actually has a much greater impact on people who invest in individual stocks, because they often hold stocks too long to avoid paying tax and, as a result, see their gains slip into losses. I don't think you should ever make investment decisions based on the tax ramifications alone. Taxes are important, but they should never be your main consideration, and both stock and fund investors make this fundamental mistake too often.

You want to realize gains rather than watch them disappear.

---

[4] John C. Bogle, *Bogle on Mutual Funds* (New York: Dell, 1994).

Shifting Funds Is Easy

Keep in mind that sometimes good performance merely means not losing as much as the market. In pursuit of this objective, it's much easier to change a portfolio made up of funds than one of individual stocks.

Assume you're back in March 2000. Technology stocks are falling out of favor (and that's a bit of an understatement). If you own 10 tech stocks, you need to make 10 agonizing decisions, which is tough to do for most investors. If, on the other hand, you own one NASDAQ fund that owns all your tech stocks, you can make one decision to sell and you're out completely.

As an alternative, consider a hypothetical situation where the market is shifting. Assume you want to move out of large-cap growth and into mid-cap value. It's very easy to simply sell one fund and buy another. It takes about five minutes. If you owned 10 large-cap growth stocks and needed to move into mid-cap value stocks, think about how long that process would take you and how much anguish you'd endure. Could the market move (down) while you were agonizing?

I should add that regardless of whether you use stocks or funds, you could lose money if you invest in the stock market. As we'll discuss later, deciding between stocks and funds is only the first part of your investment policy. A look at how to invest in these options is also necessary.

Unmanaged vs. Managed Funds

When people think of mutual funds, they usually think of actively managed funds. This means that the fund has a manager who constantly looks for unique opportunities to buy and sell stocks. Investors pool their money, and the manager of the fund purchases equity shares in various companies. Managers try to beat the market by looking for special situations where they think certain stocks will outperform the market. If the fund does much better or much worse than the overall market, it's a result of the fund manager's abilities. Most people who own funds own actively managed funds.

Index funds and ETFs are different animals altogether because they're unmanaged. This means the manager doesn't try to pick stocks that will beat the market. Index funds and ETFs seek to replicate the returns of the market or index they track. They do this by investing in the shares of companies held by an index. The fund holds onto those stocks as long as they're held in the index. If and when the index substitutes one stock for another, that's the only time your index fund or ETF makes a change in its holdings.

Today you can buy mutual funds and ETFs for almost every index: the S&P 500, the Dow Jones Industrial Average, NASDAQ, and so on. If you want to own all the companies that make up the S&P 500, you can either buy shares in each of the 500 companies (and pay all those transaction fees and commissions) or you buy one fund that holds all 500 stocks, which is easier and less expensive.

People are usually attracted to index funds and ETFs because they have low expenses. People who only want to capture the return of a certain index and not worry about the added risk of individual companies should be interested in these index products.

Open-End Funds: Pig in a Poke?

Both actively managed funds and index funds can be open-ended.

Most of the funds you know of are open-ended. This means that when an investor wants to sell her shares, she notifies the fund. The fund must redeem the investor's shares. The fund either uses the new money that came in from new investors, or sells off shares of stock held in the portfolio so the investor can be sent the equivalent of the value of her shares on the day she wants to cash out.

When a new investor wants to invest in the fund, he sends the fund a check. The manager takes the money and buys more stocks, keeps the money in a money market, or uses the proceeds to pay off other investors who are withdrawing their money from the fund. An open-end fund can keep taking in money forever. As the money comes in, the fund grows in size and simply makes more investments.

The value of every open-end fund is calculated at the end of the trading day by adding up the values of all the shares owned by the fund, then dividing this sum by the total outstanding shares.

For example, if you took a small fund and found that at the end of the day, the total value of the shares it held was $120 and the fund had a total of 10 shares outstanding, the value of each share would be $12. Again, this value is calculated at the close of trading (4 P.M. EST) daily and is calculated only once every day.

For those who own shares to cash in, they have to give their orders to sell prior to 4 P.M. EST. The value of the fund is calculated *after* 4 P.M. So they give the order to sell not knowing exactly what price they'll receive. That's the way it works with all open-end mutual funds.

Mutual Fund–Late Trading and Other Heinous Crimes against Humanity

For the vast majority who play fair, investors buy funds not knowing exactly what price they'll pay per share of the fund. But not everyone plays fair all the time. As of this writing, the media continues to level a great deal of criticism toward mutual funds because of late trading and other activities. Let's take a minute to explain what the problems are and who they affect.

There are two major problems associated with the recent mutual fund scandal. First, some fund managers engaged in the unethical trading of their own funds. They bought and sold—like day traders. This is clearly unethical, but unfortunately it's not a violation of the law. These people were speculating, and no one knows if they made money or lost money doing this. The effect on shareholders could be that it increased the expense on an annual basis, but nobody really knows for sure.

A much more egregious behavior is late trading. This is unethical *and* illegal. Basically, when a fund manager engages in this activity he buys a fund—or allows someone else to do so—*after* trading hours. As you know, funds are priced after the market closes and the law states that when you buy or sell a fund, you do so at the next day's closing price. What these people did was buy or sell the fund after the close at the earlier day's price. How did this benefit anyone?

Well, most of the funds that we know were involved in late trading were international funds. Let's say an international fund that owns European stocks closed at $10 per share on Monday. If the manager waits to buy shares on Monday night, he could see what's happening in the European markets on Tuesday because of the time zone difference. If the manager saw the European markets going up strongly on Tuesday, he could buy the fund on Monday night at the Monday close price and sell the next day for a profit because he already had an indication of what the market was going to do. This is illegal, as I said before.

So how much does this affect you and how can you avoid the problem? One junior professor estimated the cost to investors at roughly .5 percent per year for those investors owning funds where the manager engaged in late trading. Many experts have taken issue with this figure and argue that it's widely exaggerated. Bottom line? Even though it looks like the financial impact is negligible, the issue of late trading is serious because it's a blow to our sense of others acting in good faith and honesty. It makes it harder to feel secure in having trust in fund managers. **You can avoid the issue by buying exchange-traded funds.** They're not mutual funds. Unlike mutual funds, the prices of ETFs are set throughout the day. As a result, the late trading problem disappears.

Closed-End Funds: More Risk, More Opportunity

The counterpart to open-end funds is closed-end funds. Like open-end funds, closed-end funds can either be actively managed or pegged to an index. All ETFs are closed-end index funds. ETFs and closed-end index funds often own the same securities as open-end index funds. The big difference between open- and closed-end funds lies in how these funds are bought and sold.

If you want to buy or sell your open-end fund, you do so directly with the company who sold you your shares. The fund company can issue an unlimited number of shares, and they must always redeem your shares when you decide to cash out.

Closed-end funds are quite another story. The number of shares a closed-end fund can issue is limited. Once the company issues shares, that's it. You want more shares? Go buy them from someone else on the exchange. In other words, shares for closed-end funds are bought and sold like stocks on the American, Chicago, or the New York stock exchanges—just like the shares of any publicly held company. If you want to sell your shares of a closed-end fund, you must find another buyer on one of these exchanges.

As a result of this limitation, the shares frequently trade at a discount or premium to their value.

How Closed-End Fund Shares Are Valued

Open-end fund shares are valued directly as a result of the assets owned by the fund. When the value of those shares rises in value, it drives the value of the fund up directly.

In a closed-end fund, if the shares it holds increase in value, it does help the price of the fund increase, but that's not the end of the story. In the case of a closed-end fund, considerations other than the value of its assets affect the value of the fund's share price. For example, if everyone who owns shares in this closed-end fund thought the fund manager was a genius and really knew how to pick stocks, they'd be tempted to hold onto those shares, and nobody would want to sell. If another investor came along who wanted to buy shares, she'd have to pay a premium for them. She'd have to pay more for the fund shares than the value of the assets. In other words, even though the value of the assets held by the fund might be only $12 per share, new investors might have to offer more than $12 to entice existing shareholders into selling their shares. This is what's known as a premium.

Likewise, if investors dump their shares of the fund because they think the manager doesn't know his assets from his liabilities, the shares of the fund could plummet even though the assets held by the fund rise in price! If the manager of a closed-end fund is held in low regard, the only way shareholders can saddle someone else with their shares is to offer them at a significant discount.

Because closed-end funds can trade at a premium or discount to their value, this adds a level of risk—and opportunity—for you as an investor. As a result, many investors stay away from closed-end funds.

However, ETFs are a unique closed-end fund. Because of the way they're structured, ETFs rarely trade at a *large* premium or discount to value.[5] To gain understanding about how this works, visit

---

[5] http://www.iShares.com/tools/premium.jhtml#

www.iShares.com. Yet as you're reading this, it's more important to understand that this is the way things are than to understand why they are that way. And because of this, you don't have to worry about your ETF trading at premiums and discounts—one less thing to worry about.

Who Offers ETFs?

Many companies offer ETFs; there are currently hundreds of choices. Barclays Global Investors invented the exchange-traded-fund concept back in 1973, and today they're the largest index investor, currently offering the greatest variety of ETFs (a total of 81 choices). If you want further information, please visit www.iShares.com.

Why Are Index Funds and ETFs Attractive?

You've learned so far that:
1. It makes sense to use equity growth to achieve long-term goals.
2. It makes sense for many investors to use funds rather than individual stocks.

Now the question remains, which funds? Actively managed or indexed?

John Bogle, founder of Vanguard Group of Investment Companies, states that most actively managed mutual funds underperform the market by 2.2 percent annually.[6] This is a result of excessive fees, high turnover, and lack of ability. If most actively managed funds underperform by that much, the results present a persuasive argument against using actively managed funds.

---

[6] John C. Bogle, *Bogle on Mutual Funds*, 170.

Why Smart People Lose a Fortune

Commenting on a handful of stellar fund managers, investment guru Peter Lynch added, "Those notable exceptions are entirely outnumbered by the run-of-the-mill fund managers, dull fund managers, plus other assorted camp followers, fuddy-duddies, and copycats hemmed in by the rules."[7]

So two of the most highly regarded individuals in the mutual fund industry feel that most actively managed funds provide low value. Maybe we should sit up and take note of that. How do you determine if an ETF or index fund is better than your fund? Visit my website at www.NealFrankle.com for an easy tool you can use.

Cost Benefit

Both index funds and ETFs have low expenses. As we saw earlier, the management expenses for domestic exchange-traded funds range from 0.15 percent to 0.25 percent, a much lower rate than your average actively managed fund that charges 1.5 percent.

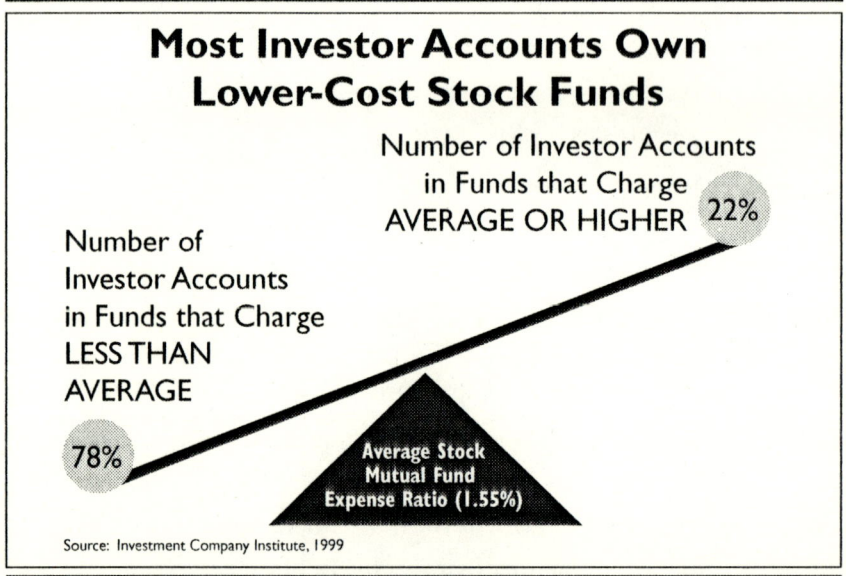

---

[7] Peter Lynch and John Rothchild, *One Up On Wall Street*.

ETFs and index funds have tax benefits as well. Because the managers do very little trading, investors don't have to worry about capital gain distributions.

How to Decide Between Index Funds and ETFs

In addition to the cost advantage mentioned above, the big benefit of ETFs over index funds is that they are traded like a stock. As a result, they can be bought and sold during the day. Investors don't need to wait for the end of the business day to know the price of the fund. Also, investors can use stop-losses, limit orders, and margins to trade ETFs and other closed-end funds.

In summary, ETFs have a great many advantages. They're inexpensive to own, you don't have to worry about huge capital gain exposure, you don't need to be concerned about premiums and discounts, and you can easily trade them during the day.

So, with all this good news, why haven't you heard of ETFs before?

Well, there's an old saying that investments are sold and not bought, and these little gems are investments that Wall Street has little incentive to sell.

Brokers earn very little commission when they sell ETFs. On top of that, the brokerage firm receives no ongoing management fee as a result of a sale. (Some large brokerage firms are starting to offer their own version of the ETFs—if you were to buy these ETFs, the firm *would* earn ongoing management fees.)

Because your broker earns almost no commission when she sells ETFs, you rarely hear her suggest them as an investment unless you bring it up. It's painful to say, but here you have an example of a great investment alternative not offered to clients because Wall Street doesn't receive enough profits by promoting it.

Many other examples exist where great alternatives have been available but not presented to clients because the clients' interests came second. I've always said that if you show me the investment portfolio of a client, I'll tell you exactly where that client gets his advice.

Having discovered the benefits of owning ETFs, some investors go overboard and vow to invest only in ETFs and never consider actively managed funds again.

This is a mistake. Even though I've explained how great index funds and ETFs are, I don't want to suggest that you should exclude actively managed mutual funds from consideration. There will be times when it's most appropriate to use actively managed mutual funds, and there will be other times when ETFs or index funds make more sense (I show you how to make that decision in chapter 9.) Your goal is to grow the money without taking undue risk, remember? That's the bottom line. You're trying to realize your goals and values. That's all that matters. You want to make smart decisions about your money so you can stop worrying and start enjoying the things that are really important to you.

I encourage you to look for the best mutual fund or index fund (or ETF) for the particular market you're in. Many times I find that an actively managed mutual fund performs better than an ETF. This can happen despite the fact that actively managed funds have higher expenses and other limitations.

Why does that happen? Well, we know that *most* funds do not outperform the market—but at any given time there will be *some* funds that do outperform.[8] The method I describe later is good at finding those funds that stand head and shoulders above the others at any particular time. Many times, this particular fund will also outperform the index. When this happens, it makes sense to invest in the fund rather than the ETF.

---

[8] Dolly Setton (ed.), "A Mutual Fund Momentum Strategy with Staying Power," *Forbes.com*, October 24, 2001, www.forbes.com/2001/10/24/1024inladviser_print.html.

I prefer to use ETFs or index funds whenever possible, but if I see that the actively managed fund has done better than the index fund, I'm not going to be a fool and insist that I'm smarter than the market. I'll always be better off by listening to the market.

Points of Interest

- When deciding between funds and individual stocks, consider your ultimate goals. Then take the course of action that will help you achieve your goals with less risk. For most people, funds are appropriate.
- Individual stocks can help you make a lot more money if you hit a home run, but they can also cause you to lose a lot more money if you strike out. Think about the potential benefits and the potential drawbacks before you decide. What could go wrong and how badly would that hurt you? If the downside of owning individual stocks is unacceptable, don't buy them.
- Because people get emotionally attached to their stocks, the process of parting with them can be difficult. As a result, individual stockholders often lose control over their investments.
- You can often reduce your capital gains tax liability by "tax loss harvesting."
- You can avoid funds that pay out higher capital gains by looking for low-turnover funds.
- Taxes are important to consider, but ultimately you're better off making solid investment decisions and paying the tax. There's no excuse for watching a gain turn into a loss just because you wanted to delay paying capital gains tax.
- You can own high-fee funds or low-fee funds. With a little investigation, you can take advantage of the lower-cost alternatives. The bottom line is value. Certainly fund investors

pay expenses, but so do individual stock investors. Consider which investment is more in line with your ultimate goals, which are much more important than the costs.
- Exchange-traded funds have the added advantage of being traded like a stock; you can buy or sell them throughout the day.
- Don't expect brokers to tell you about ETFs or index funds. They don't have much financial incentive to educate you about these alternatives.

Exercises

1. In mid-December call your fund companies to determine how much capital gains were declared on funds held in your taxable accounts for the entire year.
2. Employ the technique outlined in this chapter to eliminate any phantom gains on which you'd otherwise have to pay tax.
3. Call your financial adviser and tax adviser. Ask why they never suggested this technique to you. While you're at it, ask your financial adviser why she never introduced you to ETFs.

Watch Out
Develop Your Market Sensitivity

"When the facts change, I change my mind. What do you do, sir?"
JOHN MAYNARD KEYNES, Economist

Throughout this book I've suggested you protect your investments by minimizing risk. Perhaps I've even harped about listening to the market. In this chapter, you'll learn what to listen for (or, put another way, how to take the market's temperature), which will give you an indicator for getting into the market when opportunity is greatest—and getting out when risk is highest.

You might be asking yourself if this is just dressing up the old adage of buy low, sell high. It isn't. I want you to buy high and sell higher. (Have you ever bought low only to see the investments go lower? When you try to buy low, it's often like trying to catch a falling knife: You're bound to get a nasty cut sooner or later.) My experience has been that nobody really knows when "low" means "lowest" or when it means "low and dropping." So invest only when you have some evidence to support your suspicion that it's safe to do so. Look for strength in a healthy market before investing.

I call this market sensitivity. Others refer to it as market timing, but I'm not fond of that term because it conjures the image of a nervous, type-A personality sitting in front of her computer, trying to predict what's going to happen next in the stock market.

Emulating that would be a mistake. With market sensitivity, you don't try to predict the market at all. By taking the market's temperature, you measure risk and invest accordingly. The market, not the investor, calls the shots. The market, not the so-called experts, tells you when to invest.

Detractors of market timing and market sensitivity methods tell you to steer clear because you won't make money 100 percent of the time. But this is disingenuous; no method makes you money all the time. No method shields you completely from the vagaries of the market—certainly not buy and hold, not asset allocation, not following Morningstar or Value Line. Unlike other methods, market sensitivity evaluates the overall market situation and helps determine what action makes most sense given the current market conditions.

A good investment method should allow you to capture most of the gains in a healthy market and avoid many of the devastating losses in a weak market. If you can get in during the early stages of a rally and get out during the early stages of a downturn, you should be able to make money, preserve your capital, and achieve what's most important to you.

The Overall Market Affects Your Money

According to William O'Neil, even if you own great stocks with growing sales and earnings, great products, and great management, "If you are wrong about the direction of the broad general market, three out of four of your stocks will slump with the market averages and you will lose money. Therefore, you need . . . a simple, reliable method to determine if you're in a bull market or a bear market."[1] That being the case, don't you think it would be helpful to understand the general health of the market prior to investing?

Yet O'Neil goes on to clearly instruct people who own mutual funds to buy and hold, which is where he and I part ways.[2] If three out of four stocks are going down in value, why hold a fund that has a high likelihood of declining? It just doesn't make sense to me.

In the introduction to this book, I told you that my own personal breakthrough with the methods I'm presenting here came

---
[1] William J. O'Neil, *How to Make Money in Stocks*, 3rd ed., 48.
[2] William J. O'Neil, *How to Make Money in Stocks*, 3rd ed., 236.

the year after my clients and I took a bath with our mutual funds in 2000, when I created the safety net strategy that ultimately saved my clients a fortune. One of the main reasons I saw for considering overall market strength when investing in funds was this very statistic: If we agree that three out of four stocks move with the general direction of the market, we should also agree that understanding the general health of the market is critical even to those who invest in mutual funds. Why? Because equity funds are made up of—you got it—equities. If three out of four stocks decline in a weak market and you own a fund made up of equities, three out of four of the stocks in your fund are probably going to decline in value, and that will bring the value of your fund down.

> *"Any plan is bad which is incapable of modification."*
> PUBLILIUS SYRUS, Philosopher

Market Sensitivity vs. Buy and Forget About It

Paying attention to the overall market every day can help you avoid crashing on the rocks. Need an illustration? Consider what would have happened to you had you invested $100,000 in the S&P Index on March 31, 2000. If your strategy was buy and forget about it, you would have seen your money shrink to $61,000 by August 30, 2002, which would have been a loss of 39 percent. If invested in the NASDAQ 100, it would have shrunk to $34,000—a loss of over 66 percent. How long will it take to make up for that? People investing with buy and forget about it are drowning.

Market sensitivity is your lifeline. Will it hold? I can't predict every possible eventuality, but I can tell what will happen to you if you don't grab onto it: You'll drown.

I can't promise that, on every trading day, taking the market's temperature and following its reading will always make you more money than buy and forget about it, but here's what I *can* demonstrate:

1. Because market sensitivity gets investors out of the market for at least part of the time, those who use it are subject to less risk.
2. One study, comparing the buy-and-forget-about-it method to buying only when the NASDAQ was above its 100-day moving average, shows that since 1972, the market-sensitive investor earned 18.9 percent—but the buy-and-forget-about-it investor earned just 11.8 percent. The figures don't include fund expenses, management fees, or taxes.[3]
3. Doug Fabian, publisher of *Maverick Advisor*, invests based on the 39-week average. Since 1980, his annualized return has beaten the buy-and-forget-about-it investors owning the Wilshire 5000 with 22 percent less risk.[4]
4. Look at the advertisement on the opposite page.

The ad doesn't reflect actual results and the use of this method doesn't guarantee investors against the possibility of loss. Since these results don't represent actual trading, they may not reflect the impact that material economic and market factors might have had.

This shows the action an investor *could* have taken had he paid attention to the general conditions of the market from January 1999 through June 2002 as reported by *Investor's Business Daily*. There's no guarantee that an investor would have achieved these results because, unlike the 100-day moving average, this method is not 100 percent mechanical.

Look at that ad again. If you're like most people, you think about how much money and heartache you could have saved had you paid attention to what the market was telling you.

---

[3] Ken Hoover, "Fund Timers Clip the Market's Edges," *Investor's Business Daily*, October 9, 2002.

[4] Ken Hoover, "Fund Timers Clip the Market's Edges."

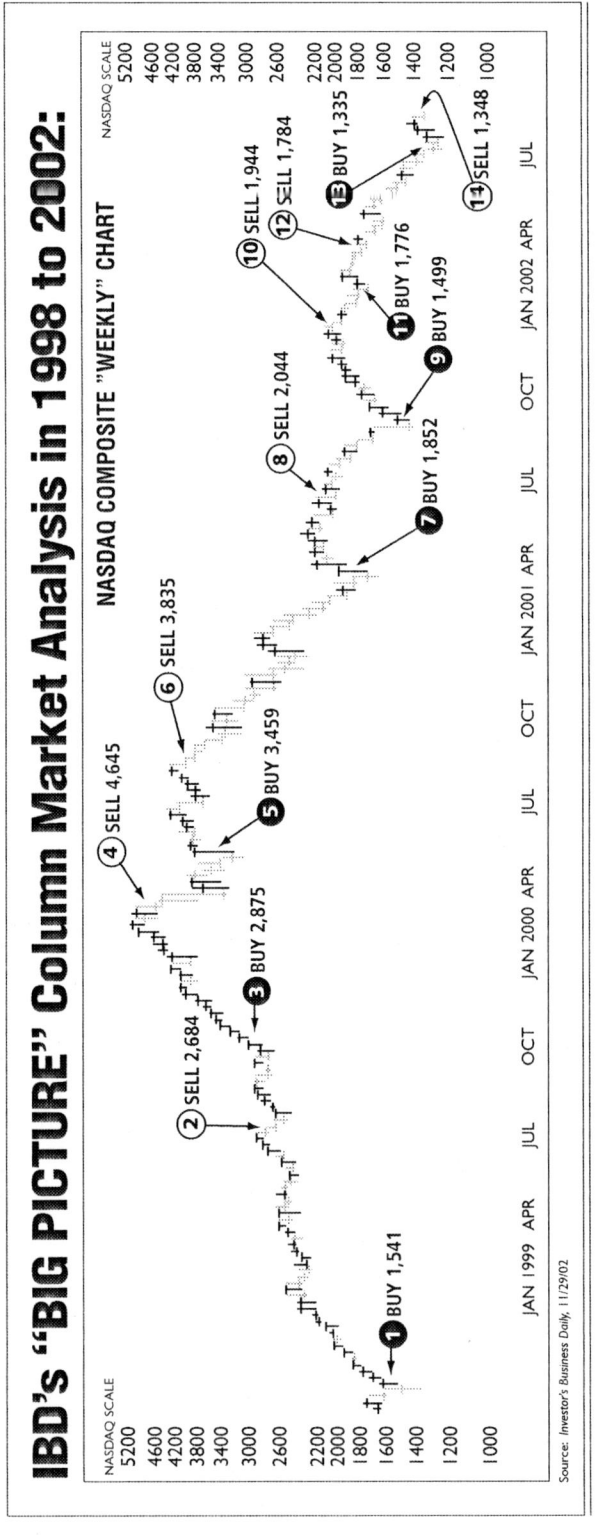

The good news is there's an easy way to access information on the health of the market. Commentary presented by *Investor's Business Daily* indicates when the market is strong and when the market is weak. The paper doesn't tell you to sell or buy, but it does analyze the general market conditions every day. The front page lets you know if the market is in a confirmed rally or downturn, and the Big Picture column usually recaps the market position every day.

Take the Market's Temperature

How can you tell if the market's in good shape? The first main ingredient of a healthy market is big players buying stocks. Seventy-five percent of all the money in the market is invested by mutual funds, insurance companies, and pension plans.[5] When these institutions invest, it's easy to see—like an elephant jumping into a bathtub. They have a lot of money to throw around, and when they do, it makes waves. You can see these waves by huge increases in trading volume for the day.

When you see one of the major indexes increase by at least 2 percent on higher volume than the previous day, this indicates institutions are buying stocks big time.[6] This is an accumulation day. Before you're ready to deem this a healthy market, you look for confirmation of the first accumulation day.

You get that confirmation if, within three to seven business days after the first accumulation day, you observe another accumulation day.[7] In this case, you have the confirmation you're looking for: the makings of a good market. These two signals together constitute institutional buying or accumulation.

For example, if the Dow trades at 10,000 and you see a day where it rises by 200 points on volume greater than the previous day, that's the first accumulation day. Then, if you see another

---

[5–7] Ken Hoover, "Fund Timers Clip the Market's Edges."

accumulation day between the third and seventh business day after the first accumulation day, you have your confirmation.

These accumulation days are critical, but by themselves they're not conclusive. In addition to accumulation days, you want to see above-average trade volume. If you see volume increase from the previous day, but the increase is on below-average volume, you can't have a lot of confidence in the market. You want volume to be very strong. You want an indication that the big buyers are convinced and committed to buying shares. You're looking for conviction, and the volume numbers are where you find that conviction—if it's there.

Volume is sometimes more important than price movement. If you observe these accumulation days on strong volume, the other required ingredient is high-quality stocks breaking out.[8] Stock market leaders should be doing well: advancing and holding onto their advance.

Who are the market leaders? Simply put, they're those stocks with great management, fantastic earnings, fabulous products, and the best performance in the market. Market leaders emerge from strong industries where a number of stocks are doing really well in terms of market performance.

If you read *Investor's Business Daily*, you'll get a sense of who the leaders are and how they're doing. In fact, the paper now makes it very easy for you. It lists the market leaders on the front page every day and it details how these leaders are holding up in the market.

Understand that without market leadership, the market will not expand. If market leaders start to break down, it's probably a great time to play defense. Also know that over half of a stock's advance stems from its group strength.[9] If you have a mutual fund whose manager invests heavily in the strongest groups, you have a good chance of making money.

[8–10] Ken Hoover, "Fund Timers Clip the Market's Edges."

Don't make the mistake of watching the old guard if you're looking for clues about today's market strength. New leaders and new leading sectors emerge with each bull market.[10] In the 1960s, airlines took off. In the late 1970s, oil companies and computer firms were hot. In the 1990s, it was the telecoms, biotechs, and Internets that caught investors' attention. Changes in industry conditions, the tax code, hikes or decreases in military spending, and interest rate changes all play their part in changing market strength.

Consider the accompanying chart. You can see that in every decade since the 1950s, the market was led by different companies

Different Eras, Different Leaders

DECADE	NEW TRENDS	STOCK WINNERS	
1960s	Vietnam War boosts military demand	Boeing	+283% in 100 wks
	Color TV mushrooms in numbers	National Video	+362% in 32 wks
1970s	Restaurant franchise growth explodes	McDonald's	+500% in 110 wks
	Mobile home parks reach the masses	Winnebago	+433% in 53 wks
	Computers reduce costs, boost output	Wang Labs	+1,400% in 141 wks
1980s	Big boom in women's work apparel	Limited	+650% in 71 wks
	2nd baby boom boosts toy sales	Coleco	+622% in 39 wks
	Software enhances worker productivity	Adobe Systems	+511% in 29 wks
1990s	HMOs spring up to cut medical costs	United Haalth	+1,240% in 203 wks
	Strong PC demand boosts chipmaking	Micron Technol.	+2,731% in 153 wks
	Internet use goes worldwide	Yahoo	+646% in 61 wks

Source: *Investor's Business Daily*, November 6, 2002

and different industries. Please notice that you don't see any companies that led one decade and followed that leadership through to the next.

Things change all the time, which is why it's usually a mistake to cling to yesterday's market darlings in the hopes of recapturing some of that luster.

Are you holding onto fallen angels, looking to them for leadership, or do you own mutual funds that do? The chances of riding Sun, Lucent, Cisco, Microsoft, Home Depot, Wal-Mart, GE, or others to huge gains are about seven to one.

"You can't have a better tomorrow if you are thinking about yesterday all the time."

CHARLES KETTERING, Electrical Engineer and Inventor

It rarely works. As a matter of fact, research on the best stocks over the past 50 years shows that only half of those former winners ever make it back to their peaks—and it takes an average of four to five years to do so in the cases when it happens. How many of those that did make it back go on to lead future markets? Only 14 percent.[11]

Look at the next set of charts. Here you see a team of some of Wall Street's favorite consumer growth stocks for most of the 1990s. They've all performed dismally since 1998. If you want to invest to grow your money, you have to do so based on what the companies are doing now, not on what they've done in the past. Watching current leaders helps you get a bead on the market; watching past winners won't give you any relevant insight into market strength.

---

[11] Ken Hoover, "Fund Timers Clip the Market's Edges."

Favorite consumer 'growth' stocks lose their luster

Since 1998, these Wall Street darlings have performed poorly—worse than the average blue-chip stock.

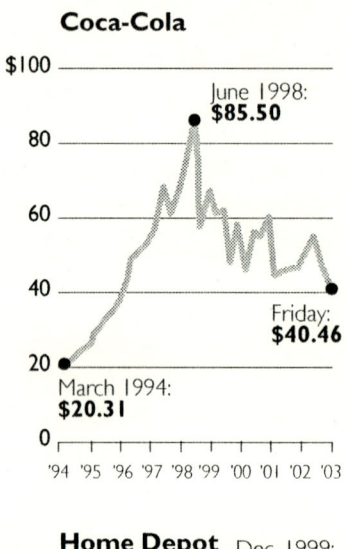

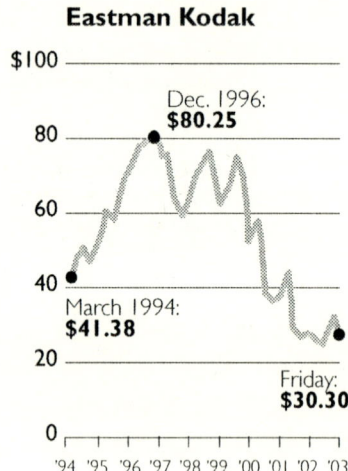

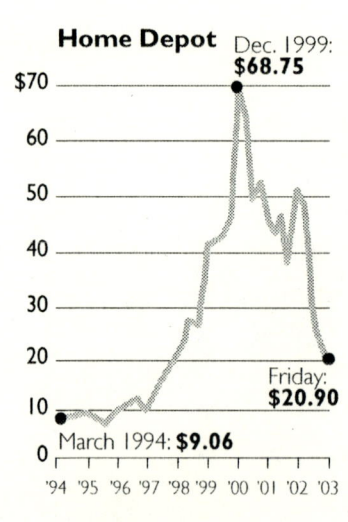

Source: *Bloomberg News*

WATCH OUT • Develop Your Market Sensitivity

So forget the past. Be open-minded to recognize new leaders—some of whom you may not be familiar with. Let's assume the market leaders are performing relatively well today. If you observe strong accumulation days, above-average trading volume, and strong market-leading stocks breaking out and doing well, you have a positive opportunity in the market.

Remember—this is not foolproof. There's no guarantee that every time you have these conditions, you'll have a good market. You must remain vigilant.

What Constitutes a Weak Market?

What about the flip side: How do you define a poor market environment?

To identify a weak market, look for distribution days. A distribution day is a decline in one of the major indexes (the Dow, the S&P, or the NASDAQ) compared to the previous business day on greater volume than the previous day.[12]

For example, assume the Dow went down by 50 points today, and it did so on higher volume than yesterday. That would qualify as a distribution day. It doesn't have to be a decline of 2 percent—any decline on higher volume will do.

If you observe four distribution days within a week or two, that usually signals the end of a rally, indicating that the tide has turned.[13] This is a good time to be very conservative and defensive. Distribution days indicate that the big players (the insurance companies, mutual funds, and pension plans, among others) are selling their stocks as fast as they can. Remember, these big players account for 75 percent of all the money invested in the better-quality leading stocks.[14] If these big boys dump stock, you'll find it difficult to make money by holding your shares or funds.

[12–13] Ken Hoover, "Fund Timers Clip the Market's Edges."
[14] William J. O'Neil and Fred Plemenos, *24 Essential Lessons for Investment Success* (New York, McGraw-Hill, 2000).

At this point, the risk outweighs the rewards. These distribution days are your main cue. If you notice distribution, carefully observe how the leading stocks are holding up at this time. If they're breaking down, *get out of the market*.

O'Neil goes into this subject in much greater detail in his books, but these two indicators are the ones I focus on daily to check the market's temperature.

Investors paying attention to these simple indicators would likely not have been subjected to the severe market losses most people suffered from March 2000 through December 2002. James Cramer, commentator of TheStreet.com and Co-Host of CNBC's *Kudlow and Cramer* said, "Anyone who read *IBD* during the first sign of the March 2000 market downturn knew it was time to sell stocks!"[15] This holds true when applied to the last 40 years as well. While certainly not predictive, an investor using these indicators would not have missed the major turns in the market.

Points of Interest

- Always keep in mind that the market's overall health will have a significant impact on how well your investments do. Learn the signs of a healthy and a poor market, and take the time to master the skills of taking the market's temperature.
- A single bear market can wipe out your financial and emotional security—don't let this happen to you.

Exercises

1. Start reading *Investor's Business Daily*.
2. Follow the general health of the market and identify the market leaders.

---

[15] Reported in the *IBD*, December 8, 2003.

Begin Now
Take 5 Steps to Market-Sensitive Investing

"A realist believes that what is done or left undone in the short run determines the long run."

SYDNEY J. HARRIS, Columnist

The simple steps I've outlined in this chapter are the ones I've used successfully with my own money and my clients' accounts. My safety net strategy blends elements of proven investment methods. Each of these steps has helped many thousands of people over an extended period of time. Many investors who paid attention to the market protected their investments from bad markets and have grown their money in good markets.[1]

Isn't that what you want to do?

In mid-2001, I started using this method for investing in mutual funds and exchange traded funds, which is probably how you'll be most interested in applying it. I admit this isn't a very long track record, but I'm not asking you to go on my track record alone. Rely on the records of the methods on which my safety net strategy is built. Even better still, rely on your own common sense. And if it helps you to know it, remember that during some of the worst years we've seen in the market, once I got them on board with this strategy, my clients have sidestepped most of the damage and got back into the market when it was appropriate to do so.[2]

To satisfy the academics, I suppose I could have waited a few more years before writing this book so I'd have a 10-year track

---

[1] William J. O'Neil, *How to Make Money in Stocks*, 3rd ed.
[2] For an updated track record, visit http://www.wealthresourcesgroup.com/1FAQs.htm.

record. But if I'd waited before I started to protect portfolios, all my clients could have been working at Flippy Burger. How long are you going to wait before you start protecting your assets?

Step 1. Take the Market's Temperature

Refer to the previous chapter for details on how to take the market's temperature. If you read the market as being strong, be ready to commit 25 percent of your account value to equities, whether in ETFs or mutual funds, depending on your acceptable level of risk.

Look for market accumulation or distribution and observe how leading stocks are holding up. If you note accumulation and also see that the market leaders are doing well, you have a green light.

Step 2. Determine Which Quadrant Is Strongest

Once you have a green light on the overall health of the market, you can commit 25 percent of your assets to investment. Now the question is, where?

You need to know which area of the market is strongest. We'll restrict our review to four quadrants because they're sufficient to take the market's temperature. They are:

Large-Cap Growth	Large-Cap Value
Small-Cap Growth	Small-Cap Value

It's easy to spot which quadrants are doing best. To get a handle on this, consult two graphs included every day in *Investor's Business Daily*.

BEGIN NOW • *Take 5 Steps to Market-Sensitive Investing*

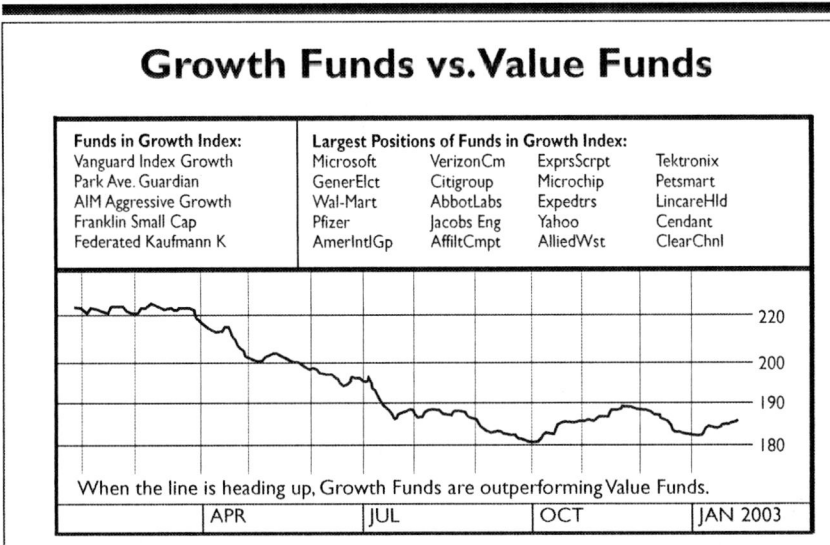

Source: *Investor's Business Daily*

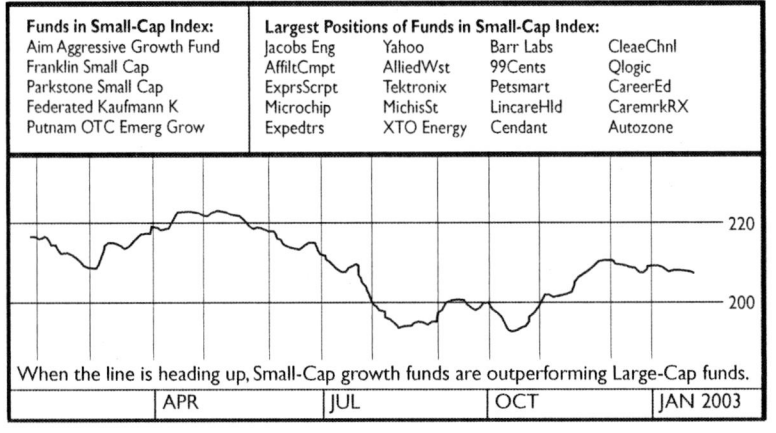

Source: *Investor's Business Daily*

Examine these graphs. The top graph shows value and growth relative to each other. The line is heading up, so growth funds are doing better than value funds.

The bottom graph shows how small-cap growth funds vs. large-cap growth funds are performing. In this example, the line is heading down, so large-cap growth funds are doing better than small-cap.

If you put this together, the strongest area of the market for our example is large-cap growth, so you'd invest 25 percent of your assets in a large-cap growth fund.

Step 3. Identify the Specific Mutual or Index Fund

There are three ways to do this:

1. Use the NoLoad Fund*X *newsletter.* It ranks all their funds for you. Simply invest in the highest-ranked fund in the moderate risk category that's also in the desired quadrant. Consult www.fundx.com for more information. While this is not the least-expensive way (you'll have to pay for an annual subscription to *NoLoad Fund*X*), it's a simple and easy method and a good approach for most do-it-yourselfers.

2. Create your own universe of funds. Keep in mind that there are over 10,000 mutual funds from which to choose. You can pare your list down by consulting the custodian of your account for a list of all no-transaction or low-transaction funds. (I strongly suggest you use one custodian, such as TD Waterhouse, to hold your funds rather than buying each one directly from the fund company. While this may cost you a bit more, it saves you a great deal of time and it's easy to track your portfolio.) As an alternative, you could subscribe to Morningstar and filter your list based on performance, manager tenure, etc. Either way, rank them as follows:

a. Calculate each fund's returns over the past 12-, 6-, 3-, and 1-month periods.
b. Multiply the 12-month return by 15 percent, the 6-month return by 25 percent, the 3-month return by 35 percent, and the 1-month return by 25 percent.
c. Add the four figures and compute the ranking.
d. Rank your universe of funds from highest to lowest score.
e. Invest 25 percent in your highest-ranking fund that's in the correct quadrant.

(Go to www.NealFrankle.com to download a nifty spreadsheet that will make these calculations for you). Notice that this process gives more weight to the short-term performance than the long-term performance.

My universe consists of funds that are moderate, conservative, inexpensive, and have a tenured manager. I use only no-load or load-waived funds. I never use sector funds. My universe of funds includes ETFs as well.

3. *Invest in an index fund or ETF that represents the correct quadrant.* You identified the correct quadrant in step 2. Simply go to www.iShares.com and search for the index fund that makes up that quadrant.

Any of these alternatives should yield fine results. The most important element is to be in the right quadrant in a strong market. The exact selection of the fund to use is less critical.

Step 4. Move Forward

Assuming the market stays intact over the following two weeks and doesn't show any significant distribution signals, do the exact same thing for the next 25 percent of your capital. Repeat the process detailed above, find the next fund, and invest again. Don't put more than 25 percent of your assets into any one fund. Subsequently purchase the number two, three, and four funds or ETFs from your universe. The exception to this is if you invest only in index funds or ETFs. In such a case, it might be appropriate to have 100 percent of your money invested in one index fund or ETF—but that may add risk.

Assuming no selling signals appear, keep doing this until all the money is invested. If the market is healthy, it will take you six weeks to be fully invested (25 percent on day one, then another 25 percent on the first day of every other week until 100 percent is invested).

Be aware that this time lag could hurt your performance. If the market took off like a rocket during the six-week period, you'd still have some money in your money market, which would not grow with the market. Don't panic, and just follow the plan. This is the price you pay for added safety.

Step 5. Sell

There are two situations in which to sell funds.

The first situation is when the market remains strong but your fund lags. Since I suggest that you hold a fund only as long as it remains in the top 25 percent of your universe of funds, this situation is easy to remedy. By simply ranking your funds every month, you can easily monitor how your funds are continuing to hold up. If your fund does drop below the top 25 percent, sell it and buy the next highest-ranked fund that you don't currently own in the correct quadrant. If you rely on the *NoLoad Fund*X* newsletter, this is even easier because they rank the funds for you.

If you invest only in ETFs and index funds, rely on the graphs shown in chapter 7. For example, if you own the large-cap growth index and you notice that small-cap growth has become stronger, simply sell your large-cap growth index fund and purchase the small-cap growth index fund.

BEGIN NOW • *Take 5 Steps to Market-Sensitive Investing*

The second situation when you should sell funds can occur when the market becomes weak as defined in chapter 8. If you're fully invested and you receive a sell indication, sell the weakest holding. Continue selling every two weeks until you're completely in cash.

Using this system, you can get conflicting signals at times. For example, you may be 75 percent invested and before you invest the last 25 percent, you might receive a sell signal. Likewise, you may have sold 50 percent of the portfolio and before you make the next sale, you may get a buy signal. Just follow the most recent signal.

To some, this might start sounding like day-trading. I assure you it's not. You do very little trading using this method. With this method, making even one transaction each month would be highly unusual. These signals are not easily triggered—it takes a big move in the market either on the upside or downside to indicate accumulation or distribution.

But even if you do get signals that quickly contradict each other, you should be very happy. Why? Because this indicates that the market is completely meshuga and can't make up its mind. Sure, it's a pain in the neck. It might drive you crazy.

But it could also save you a fortune.

Such a situation indicates danger and you should proceed with extreme caution. The market is telling you to be careful—and you have the tools to decipher this message. This just makes sense. Remember, the alternative to paying attention to the market and taking its temperature is to stand by and watch your account values melt like a snowman in July.

---

*"Once you embrace unpleasant news,
not as a negative but as evidence of a need for change,
you aren't defeated by it. You're learning from it."*

BILL GATES, Chairman, Microsoft

It doesn't really matter what you like or dislike. If you've gotten this far in the book, you should know that the market is your boss. Your job is to listen. **The market says, "Jump," and you ask, "How high?" That's all there is to managing money using my safety net strategy.**

So, you like what you've read here, but you don't know how to start implementing these ideas. Perhaps you have losses—and you think you want to hold on "until the stocks and funds come back" before making any changes.

Nip that in the bud immediately.

If you agree that the methods you've learned here are good, why wait? If you're in funds now and the system tells you to sell, you should sell immediately.

If the market is positive and you're holding funds that aren't in the desired area of the market, upgrade immediately to the appropriate funds. It's always the right time to do the right thing.

"The path to success is to take massive, determined action."

ANTHONY ROBBINS, Peak Performance Coach

Even if you have a large portion of your assets in one stock, I suggest you upgrade immediately to this system. Yes, you pay income tax—but you protect your future and take less risk going forward.

I know this is easier to say than to do. Some folks refuse to sell shares because they don't want to pay a huge tax in one year. I understand, so while I still think it probably makes more sense to sell *all* the shares, here's a compromise.

Assume you have $8 million in XYZ stock trading at $63. Place laddered stops on those shares. For the first million dollars worth of stock, place a stop at $60. For the next two million, place a stop at $57. Continue this until you've protected all your shares. In this case, you're not stopped out of all your shares at one time, but you do protect all your capital.

If the share price moves up, ratchet the stop prices up accordingly. You can also place laddered limit orders to sell once the stock hits higher prices. For the same example, you could sell a certain number of shares once the price hits $65, another portion of shares once the stock breaches $68, and so on.

Doing this is not as emotionally upsetting as pulling the plug on all your stocks at one time, but either way it's very important to have a plan to protect your assets so you can achieve what's important to you in life.

Points of Interest

- Pay close attention to the general health of the market. Once you see evidence of accumulation, buy the strongest fund or ETF in the strongest area of the market.
- Follow the system. Sell if you see evidence of distribution. Buy if you see evidence of accumulation.
- Don't be upset by reversals. If your investment method has you buy and then sell shortly thereafter, it indicates that the market is uncommitted. In such a case, you're better off to execute the transactions and to have a reliable system than to try to outsmart the market or watch your money evaporate.
- As we saw earlier, taking the market's temperature certainly could have helped many investors avoid the catastrophic 2000 through 2002 market and take advantage of the bull market

that started in March 2003.[3] However, I'll admit that implementing this requires a bit of time and patience. It does involve some work. Not much, but some. You should be able to keep tabs on the market's overall health in 20 to 30 minutes a day.

▸ Don't wait to get started.

Exercises

1. Review this chapter and decide which funds you want to include in your universe of funds or use NoLoad Fund*X .
2. Rank your funds each month according to the instructions you learned on the preceding pages.
3. Make decisions to invest or not.
4. Compare your results to what would have happened with a buy-and-forget-about-it strategy. You'll be happy you made the switch.

---

[3] During 2000 through 2003, there were a number of instances when this system signaled it was time to get back into the market, only to reverse itself shortly thereafter. People following those signals lost some money but did avoid making the catastrophic mistake of doing nothing while their accounts evaporated. Even with these false positives, people following this method did far better than those investors who bought and held during that time period.

Invest Wisely
Use This Method to Succeed with the Market

"If things start going wrong, having a consistent approach prevents panic. There's nothing worse than entering an important situation and changing the way you do things because of the pressure."
SHANE MURPHY, Olympic Sports Psychologist

In this book, I hope to have turned a lot of financial "wisdom" on its head. For the sake of reinforcement and just on general principle, let's review . . .

Your Emotions

Emotions can rule and ruin your investments by paralyzing you so you don't sell them when you should, and that reluctance to sell often turns tiny losses into huge losses.

The method presented in this book takes care of that problem for the most part. When the market signals weakness, this method tells you to sell. It doesn't require that you hold on as your ship sinks into the deep, deep blue. By sticking to this method, you take action that coincides with what's really happening in the world—which will reduce stress and protect your capital. Happy day!

Of course, you're delighted as this method pulls you out of the market into the safety and warmth of the good ole money market during a bad market.

When this system sees market strength, it tells you to *incrementally* invest. But if the market has been very weak recently, you may not feel so warm and fuzzy about going back in. You'll be like the young fledgling, afraid to leave the safety of the warm nest.

At that point, you may prefer to stay in the safe shelter of the money market, but again you'll be better off if you follow the method rather than your emotions.

Most of my clients allow me to implement this method and are very happy doing so. One of my clients, Bill, took exception. Of course, Bill was delighted that the safety net strategy helped him avoid most of the market damage in 2002, but when the market signaled strength in March 2003, he refused to invest. From March 2003 through June 2003, the market rose 20 percent, and this client missed those gains.

There will be other times when the market soars while the method here requires that you stay invested in the money market. You may be impatient and want to rush in when the system calls for you to remain on alert. You may also find yourself hesitant, like Bill, when you need to go forward. Please understand that in any case, if you give in to these feelings, you're left with no system at all. You're investing purely based on your emotions at this point. You're better served by reminding yourself what's most important about money to you. If that includes safety, less stress, flexibility, and freedom, just stick to the system.

Make no mistake—sticking to this system takes discipline. You have a natural preference to do what feels good rather than what's good for you. You must be willing to counter that instinct, or no investment method will help.

Asset Allocation

Asset allocation as a way to improve performance is a myth. It calls for you to hold a variety of investments in bonds and equities regardless of what the market is doing. Some of these might perform quite well, while others significantly underperform. But I've never seen it demonstrated that asset allocation can help investors achieve their goals. Why arbitrarily invest in areas that are weak?

Instead, the method presented here instructs you to invest in the strongest areas of the market—but only when the overall market demonstrates strength. Doesn't this make more sense to you?

Buy and Hold

You now realize that this may be a great strategy for your broker and for the mutual fund industry, but not for you. You see how dangerous this can be. The strategy presented here makes your investments audition for a role in your financial play—every morning. If the market isn't right or the fund isn't performing, you have the tools to fire the cast and hire new actors.

The Media

Ignore ads and advisers' research. Instead, rely on the market for direction. Don't try to forecast where the market is going (based on the economy, current events, or anything else). Just let the market interpret what's happening in the economy and in the world. Allow the market to tell you how important some event is—all you have to do is listen, and the market will tell you.

> "Success is more a function of consistent common sense than it is of genius."
> AN WANG, Inventor and Industrialist

Market Sensitivity

Investors are told to ignore the market because nobody can interpret it perfectly. However, just because you don't make every call right, does that mean you shouldn't protect yourself? Seat belts don't protect you against every accident—does that mean you shouldn't wear them? Of course you should.

Certainly, even if you rely on the methods presented here, you'll lose money at some time or another. On top of that, sometimes you're out of the market and miss out on some gains. These failures can't be helped.

The good news is that these aren't the kinds of mistakes that will lead you to employment at Flippy Burger at the age of 74. They're simply the price of safety. You must avoid the catastrophic mistakes and not ride your money into the ground.

Market Leadership

Most investors never think about market leadership, yet to folks who take advantage of this method, it's critical. First, savvy investors understand that no market is strong if it doesn't have strong leaders. Second, they understand that market leadership changes constantly. Each era brings its own emerging technologies and trends; to expect yesterday's market darlings to lead the market in the future is dangerous and groundless. Last, the role of changing leadership helps explain why funds have to perform well in the relative short term in order to be on your investment team. Three- and five-year track records just aren't relevant. For a fund manager to make money for you today, she has to invest in the strongest area of the market—period.

You Will Be Tempted to Abandon Your Investment Methodology. Ignore That Temptation.

Imagine you and your neighbor each invest $100,000 on January 1. Picture yourself using a system that pays attention to risk and your neighbor buys the NASDAQ index and forgets about it. Assume you lose 6 percent in year one. Your $100,000 shrivels to $94,000. Your neighbor does much worse. His $100,000 investment melts to $67,000, but that doesn't make you feel any better. You start to worry about your losses. It gets worse. Assume that in the following year you make 20 percent while your smarty-pants neighbor, who invests in the NASDAQ, sees his money increase by over 50 percent. You might feel like a dunce for not being completely invested in the NASDAQ at this point. You might be tempted to throw out this method and curse the day you read this book. I implore you to slow down and take a good look at what is really happening.

Keep in mind that your neighbor who lost 33 percent in year one needs a gain of 50 percent to make up for it just to get back his initial $100,000. If you examine the facts, the person who is able to sidestep the major market losses doesn't need to make huge gains (and take huge risks) in order to do well. Even after the fabulous market returns for the NASDAQ in year two, the buy-and-hold investor is still well behind the market-sensitive investor in this example. Please examine the chart below.

And remember, the goal is to stop worrying about your money forever. The goal is to spend time on things that matter to you most and to have less stress and more freedom. There is no system that makes big money in good times and bad. If you try to have your cake and eat it, too, the chances are, you'll end up with neither.

	Market Sensitive Start Value: $100,000	**Buy & Hold - NASDAQ** Start Value: $100,000
Year One, Balance	$94,000	$67,000
Year Two, Balance	$112,800	$100,500

Still don't believe that you need to stick to an investment method that evaluates risk?

The world's best investors and traders do. In *The New Market Wizards*, author Jack Schwager interviewed those top investors and traders in America who had consistent and phenomenal results. Schwager came to some interesting conclusions: he states that all these exceptional investors used very different types of systems and methods. Some were fundamentalists, others used only technical analysis, and others combined those two methodologies. Some people looked at two days as long-term, while others considered two months to be short-term. Despite the wide variety of investment styles, he found that certain principles were common to all the successful investors.

What were the common threads of all 40 interviewees? Each person had a methodology that was consistent with his or her personality, and they stuck with it. Schwager also said that every person he interviewed felt that money management (risk management) was even more important than how they invested. In other words, successful investors all had ways to control risk and minimize losses. They all had tools in place to keep them from experiencing catastrophic losses.[1]

Let's apply this to you. Assume you manage your money as described in chapter 9. Assume you're the kind of person who wants to avoid "the big mistake." You don't want to suffer huge losses and you want to make good returns in good markets. Perfecto! Stick to what you've got.

If you switch to buying and holding, ignoring the overall health of the market, or asset allocation, you could be making that change at exactly the wrong time. You could be doing it just in time to catch the next leg *down*.

---

[1] Jack D. Schwager *The New Market Wizards* (New York, HarperCollins: 1992).

It's critical that you know yourself. As an investor, you've *got* to know your limitations! Make sure your investment strategy is suited to your personality. If it's not, you'll throw your methodology out the first time your emotions clash with your results. This is not just my opinion, but what Mr. Schwager discovered from interviewing the world's best investors and traders. If you're averse to risk, make sure you invest in such a way to protect yourself from stormy markets.

Points of Interest

- Please understand that nothing is perfect. Using the methods detailed in this book won't shield you from losing money always. To make matters worse, sometimes, using the methods outlined here will force you to sit on the sidelines while others are making money. Given that, it still makes sense to implement the ideas presented here if your goals are to stop worrying about your investments and avoid big mistakes. For such a person, the system I provide for you is still the best alternative.

- Asset allocation and buy and hold can lead to catastrophic losses because each fail to recognize the effect the overall market has on your investments. This is like driving 35 miles per hour in a 35 mile per hour zone – when a hurricane is right behind you.

- Once you implement this strategy stick to it even though you will be tempted to stray. You'll be glad you did.

Exercises

1. You created a list of "what's important about money" in Chapter 1. Review that list again.
2. Write down all the pros and cons to investing based on: BUY & HOLD, ASSET ALLOCATION and the SAFETY NET strategy presented here.
3. Make a decision how you are going to invest to achieve the things that matter most to you and then stick to that decision no matter what.

Afterword

"The greatest and noblest pleasure which men can have in this world is to discover new truths; and the next is to shake off old prejudices."
FREDERICK THE GREAT, King of Prussia

To make good investments, you first need to understand the environment in which you're operating: It changes. You may not like it, and the mutual fund companies may want you to ignore it, but it does change—and when you don't pay attention, you lose money.

You now have the tools you need to track these changes. You can use these tools to safeguard your money in bad markets and take advantage of opportunities as the market strengthens. With what you now know, you can either invest and manage your own investments or find someone who'll do this for you.

You might decide that this approach makes a lot of sense, but you don't have time or interest in doing this yourself. If so, please follow the guidance offered in chapter 5 for finding a trustworthy adviser to help you implement a safety net strategy.

"If we all did the things we are capable of doing, we would literally astound ourselves."
THOMAS EDISON, INVENTOR

You're intelligent and you've been successful in other areas of your life—there's no reason to believe you won't be successful at this, as well.

Why do smart people like you lose a fortune and why won't your broker tell you what to do about it? Now you know. Armed with your new understanding of how markets and investments work, I know you'll be successful in aligning your investments with what's most important to you and your family, as well as investing wisely to protect your wealth while making the most of the myriad opportunities the market presents.

You have my best wishes—and my best method. Make the most of it! I'd love to hear how it goes for you. Please contact me with your success stories at Neal@NealFrankle.com.

Appendix A
Select Bibliography and Suggested Reading

Baer, Gregory Arthur, and Gary Gensler. *The Great Mutual Fund Trap.* New York: Broadway, 2002.

Bogle, John C. *Bogle on Mutual Funds.* New York: Dell, 1994.

Bogle, John C. *Common Sense on Mutual Funds.* New York: John Wiley & Sons, 2000.

Darvas, Nicolas. *How I Made $2,000,000 in the Stock Market.* New York: Lyle Stuart, 1986.

Gastineau, Gary L. *The Exchange-Traded Funds Manual.* New York: John Wiley & Sons, 2002.

IndexFunds.com. *Exchange Traded Funds.* New York: John Wiley & Sons, 2001.

Jones, Charles P. *Mutual Funds.* New York: Financial Times Prentice Hall, 2002.

Lefevre, Edwin. *Reminiscences of a Stock Operator.* New York: John Wiley & Sons, 1994.

Livermore, Jesse. *How to Trade in Stocks.* Greenville, SC: Traders Press, 2001.

Loeb, Gerald M. *The Battle for Investment Survival.* Burlington, VT: Fraser, 1995.

Lynch, Peter, and John Rothchild. *Beating the Street.* New York: Simon & Schuster, 1994.

Lynch, Peter, and John Rothchild. *One Up on Wall Street.* New York: Penguin USA, 1990.

McClatchy, Will, and IndexFunds.com. *Strategies for Investment Success.* New York: John Wiley & Sons, 2002.

O'Higgins, Michael B., and John Downes. *Beating the Dow.* New York: HarperBusiness, 2000.

O'Higgins, Michael B., and John McCarty. *Beating the Dow with Bonds.* New York: HarperBusiness, 1999.

O'Neil, William J. *How to Make Money in Stocks*, New York: McGraw-Hill, 1991.

O'Neil, William J. *How to Make Money in Stocks*, 3rd ed. New York: McGraw-Hill, 2002.

O'Neil, William J. *24 Essential Lessons for Investment Success.* New York: McGraw-Hill, 2000.

O'Shaughnessy, James P. *What Works on Wall Street.* New York: McGraw-Hill, 1997.

Schwager, Jack D. *Market Wizards.* New York: HarperCollins, 1993.

Schwager, Jack D. *The New Market Wizards.* New York: HarperCollins, 1992.

Sethna, Dhun H. *Investing Smart.* New York: McGraw-Hill, 1997.

Shefrin, Hersh. *Beyond Greed and Fear.* New York: Oxford University Press, 2002.

Zweig, Martin. *Martin Zweig's Winning on Wall Street.* New York: Warner, 1997.

Appendix B
How Bonds Work

Think of bonds as a loan. When a company issues bonds, it borrows money from investors like you and me. The company promises to pay the investors a stated annual interest and, at some future date, repay the loan. Bonds usually pay interest every six months.

When a company issues bonds, they have a debt that must be repaid. With common shares, the company makes no promises to the investor whatsoever.

For example, consider Acme Vacuum Cleaner Company. Remember the company's owner, Mrs. Simon? She has a great idea for making a new vacuum cleaner, but she needs $100,000 to build a new factory. Assume you have $100,000 burning a hole in your pocket. The owner of Acme can raise money by selling you shares in the company or by issuing you bonds.

For this example, assume the company issues a 10 percent bond that matures July 1, 2012. Ten percent is an attractive rate. You do some checking and find that high-quality companies are able to borrow money from investors at 6 percent. Why is Acme willing to pay you 10 percent? Because the Acme Vacuum Cleaner Company is not exactly General Motors. Acme is much smaller and a greater risk. Acme might not make it. If they go out of business, the bondholders could lose their entire investment. So in order to entice you (the investor) into loaning them money, Acme must offer you higher rates.

If you invest $100,000 in this bond, you'll receive $5,000 every July and $5,000 every January until the bond matures. Once the bond matures (July 1, 2012), the company must pay you back your $100,000.

Advantages to Bonds

To an investor, bonds have certain advantages:
1. You know how much your income is and when to expect it.
2. You know that when the bond matures you'll receive your principal back.

Keep in mind that you can always sell a bond before it matures, but if you do, you may receive either more *or less* than you invested originally. If you want to sell your bond prior to maturity, you must find someone interested in buying. The issuing company may reserve the right to buy the bond back from you prior to maturity (this is known as a call feature) but you can't force them to do so.

Maturity Date

When the bond matures, you'll receive your principal back. That is, of course, if the company has the money. If the business goes bankrupt, you could lose the interest income and the original principal—100 percent down the drain.

But for all intents and purposes, let's say the company is very stable, safe, and profitable. Assume you feel pretty comfortable that you're going to get your interest every six months and your capital back at the end of the loan period.

Disadvantages

Bonds have disadvantages as well. First, they give the investor no hedge against inflation. You know the interest you're going to receive—and you won't get a penny more. The best possible scenario is the company will live up to its promises. The only "surprise" you might get is if the company runs into difficulty and you receive less than promised at the maturity date.

Second, the values of a bond may fluctuate over the course of the loan. For example, in the first year, if the company has no profit after paying their costs and wages, they still owe you (the bondholder) the 10 percent—or $10,000. They have to find the money somewhere or face default and possible bankruptcy. If the bondholders aren't paid, the value of the bonds plummets because no one wants bonds that don't pay interest.

Assume the company finds the money to pay you. Remember, they didn't make any profit this first year so they probably "found" the money by asking the top employees to forgo bonuses or compensation. In this case, no money is left over for anyone else. You, as a bondholder, don't really care because you received what was promised to you. You might be a bit concerned about the company's ability to repay you in the future since they didn't pay you from earnings. As a result, you might sell the bonds.

If you sell them, you might get less than you paid for them since the "market" knows the company doesn't have a profitable business. Potential buyers know the company may not be able to make the interest payments in the future. This lack of certainty about the company's ability to pay their obligations reduces the value of the bonds.

In year two, the company makes $10,000 in profit after all expenses. This $10,000 goes to you, the bondholder. Again, nothing is left to pay anyone else. Again, you don't care. Since the company fulfilled its obligations and is profitable, the "market" knows the bonds are solid. If you decide to sell your bonds in year two (assuming interest rates stay the same), you have a good chance of selling them for what you paid for them.

In year three, the company earns a profit of $100,000. How much do you as the bondholder receive? You guessed it—$10,000. Who gets the other $90,000? Not you—maybe the stockholders.

In year three, the bond continues to perform as promised. The company is profitable now and investors expect interest payments to continue with little risk. As a result, the value of the bonds probably won't change much assuming interest rates remain stable. Keep in mind that the value of any investment is driven by the income the investment brings to the owners—either in the present or in the future. Since the income didn't (and won't) go up, the value of the bond stays constant in our example—if all other things remain constant.

Common Misconceptions

Bonds are generally considered safe in the short run because the issuing company has a legal obligation to pay the bondholders their interest and principal. Over the life of the investment, however, bonds don't provide any growth. The only return the investor can reasonably expect to receive is the interest income. And if things go wrong, bondholders can lose everything.

On top of the business risk associated with bonds, they can fluctuate in value as interest rates change. Look at the table below, again covering a three-year period:

YEAR		INVESTED	PREVAILING INTEREST RATE	INTEREST RECEIVED	VALUE OF LARRY'S INVESTMENT
1	Larry	$100,000	10%	$10,000	$100,000
2	Moe	$100,000	5%	$5,000	$200,000
3	Curly	$100,000	20%	$20,000	$50,000

Let's assume that in year one, Larry buys a bond. He invests $100,000 at 10 percent and receives $10,000 in interest every year. The company will continue paying 10 percent on this bond until it's either called or until it matures.

APPENDIX B • How Bonds Work

In year two, interest rates have declined. A new $100,000 investment in year two returns only $5,000 in interest. Why? Maybe the economy is slow—it doesn't matter why. If Moe comes along in year two and wants to buy a bond, he can get only 5 percent. But Larry still receives $10,000 on his $100,000 investment.

Moe calls Larry and offers him $100,000 for his bond. Larry tells Moe to take a hike. (He'd sooner be poked in the eye.) If Larry were to accept the offer, he'd have to reinvest his $100,000, and since rates have dropped, Larry would be able to earn only $5,000 interest on his $100,000. If Moe really wants Larry's bond, what would he have to pay Larry in order to get him to agree to sell it?

Well, since Larry would have to invest $200,000 to re-create the $10,000 in interest he's already receiving, Moe would have to pay $200,000 in order to entice Larry into selling the bond. In other words, because interest rates changed, the value of the existing bonds changed.

Now assume that in year three, interest rates shoot way up. If rates are 20 percent, Curly would have to invest only $50,000 to generate the same interest that Larry generates with his $100,000. How much would Curly be willing to pay for Larry's bond? You got it: $50,000.

A more precise study was done by Eric Schurenberg. If you examine his chart, you'll see how even small changes in interest rates impact the value of bonds.

If interest rates rise...	Bond prices will fall...				
Amount of Increase	Maturity: 1 yr	3 yrs	7 yrs	10 yrs	20yrs
0.5%	−0.5%	−1.3%	−2.7%	−3.6%	−5.3%
1.0	−0.9	−2.6	−5.4	−6.9	−10.3
1.5	−1.4	−3.9	−7.9	−10.2	−14.8
2.0	−1.9	−5.2	−10.4	−13.3	−19.1
2.5	−2.3	−6.4	−12.8	−16.3	−23.0

Source: "401(k) Take Charge of Your Future" by Eric Schurenberg

If interest rates fall ...	Bond prices will rise ...				
Amount of decrease	Maturity: 1 yr	3 yrs	7 yrs	10 yrs	20yrs
0.5%	0.5%	1.4%	2.8%	3.7%	5.8%
1.0	1.0	2.7	5.7	7.6	12.0
1.5	1.4	4.1	8.8	11.7	18.8
2.0	1.9	5.6	11.9	16.0	26.2
2.5	2.5	7.0	15.1	20.4	34.2

Source: "401(k) Take Charge of Your Future" by Eric Schurenberg

Now you understand how market interest rates impact the value of bonds and why the value of your bond doesn't stay constant. You also understand that over time, bonds don't offer you any inflation adjustments, and as a result may be a dangerous investment to rely on in your retirement years.

Appendix C
How Equities Work

Common Shares

When you buy stocks, you own a (small) percentage of a company or business. And when you own a business, there are risks and rewards.

Business Risk

One risk of owning shares in a company is that the company's business may fail—this is called business risk. If the company is unable to deliver profits to the owners, the value of the company (and its shares) falls. To make matters worse, if the company you invest in is unable to pay its debts, the company's shares will *really* decline in value. This is because potential buyers of the shares are afraid the company is insolvent and in danger of going under. If you own shares in such a company, you might be a very unhappy camper.

On the other hand, you could own shares in a very profitable company and the value of the shares could still decline rapidly. This could happen if potential buyers of the shares have low expectations for the company in the future.

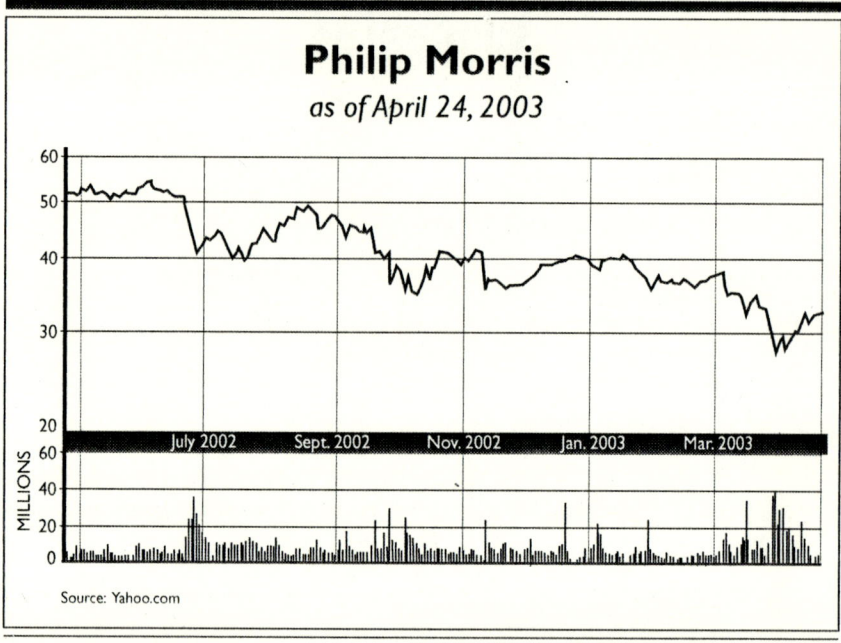

Observe what happened to the share price of Philip Morris since July 2002. Even though the company had big profits, the stock price fell apart as smokers started winning lawsuits. Investors expected Philip Morris' future to dim, so the share price fell even though current earnings were healthy.

Market Risk

Even great companies' share prices can run into trouble if the general market is sick. All stocks are subject to this risk. Investors may expect great things for the company's future, but if the overall health of the market is poor, the stock may fall. This is referred to as market risk, and it's the reason why three out of four stocks move in the general direction of the market.

APPENDIX C • *How Equities Work*

Reward

Enough bad news. Many companies are profitable, and over time, they can either reinvest the profits in the business or pay those profits to the owners of the shares (in the form of dividends)—or a combination of the two. Those companies that earn profits and reinvest can grow bigger. As they reinvest in their own business, their assets grow. As their assets grow, their ability to generate even more income grows, and so does the value of the company. As a result, the shares you own in that company increase in value.

Remember the hypothetical Acme Vacuum Cleaner Company? You may recall that the owner needs money to build a new factory, and to raise that money, she can either sell bonds or issue shares.

When the owner sells shares, she trades a portion of the ownership of the company for cash. She then takes the cash and invests in the factory. She doesn't promise the shareholders anything, but if the company is successful, the people who own shares receive a percentage of that success. This is in contrast to bondholders, where the company only promises to repay interest and principal to the investor.

In the first year, you may recall that the company has no profit and has trouble making interest payments to the bondholders. The value of the company's stock is low at this point. After all, if the company can't even pay its creditors, how can they pay their owners anything? In fact, the only thing that gives the shares any value at all is the hope that the company will be profitable in the future.

In year two, Acme did not show stellar performance—the company had just enough money to pay the bondholders and nothing left for the common shareholders. The overall health of the company did improve, but like the first year, all the stockholders have is the hope that the company will be profitable in the future: That hope is the only thing that gives the shares any value.

In year three, Acme is very profitable: $90,000 after all expenses (including bond interest) is paid. The $90,000 can be paid to the shareholders in the form of a nice dividend check or in the form of reinvestment in the vacuum factory. Either way, the shares are worth big money now. The market knows the company has turned the corner and produced stellar profits. Potential buyers fall over themselves trying to buy the stock at the current price because they expect the company to continue being very profitable and one day paying hefty dividends. As a result, these potential buyers bid the price of the shares up as they fight each other to buy. You can expect to see the value of your investment in Acme skyrocket at that point.

Appendix D
How Mutual Funds Work

A mutual fund collects investors' assets from all over the country, and sometimes throughout the world. All the money is pooled together and the manager of the fund decides what to buy and sell. In exchange for this service, the fund company collects fees. If the fund company manages many individual mutual funds, the company is referred to as a fund family.

Mutual fund managers are responsible for watching your money. They're charged with doing the research and making the decisions. They and their research team work for you on a full-time basis. This, theoretically, alleviates the need for you to spend your entire day on investment research and work—and saves you the heartache of making decisions.

Types of Funds

Some funds, called equity funds, invest only in equities. Other funds—called bond funds—invest only in bonds.

Some equity funds invest only in small companies' stock, others invest only in companies that mine gold or other precious metals, and still others invest only in technology companies.

Income funds invest in corporate or government bonds; they hold little or no equity shares.

In the financial services delicatessen, the balanced fund is goulash, offering a combo of delectable bonds and stocks. People buy these funds because they want some income and a little bit of growth—but a lot of safety.

Different funds have different objectives, as well. If your objective is to invest in companies that are growing rapidly, look for a great growth fund. If you're interested in owning companies whose shares are currently considered bargain basement prices, look for a value fund.

Mutual fund companies also offer investors money market accounts. The value of these shares doesn't normally fluctuate at all, and it's also very liquid. But you earn very little interest and these accounts aren't insured by the FDIC. Still, money markets are usually considered a safe harbor in rocky markets. It's extremely rare for investors to experience capital fluctuation when they park their money in money market accounts at a mutual fund.

How Do Funds Work?

The fund's mission is to make money for the investors, and it does so in three ways:

1. The fund may hold stocks (which pay a dividend) or bonds (which pay interest). During the year, as the dividends accumulate, the value of the fund increases. Periodically during the year, the fund declares a dividend to pay out these accumulated dividends and interest.

2. The fund may sell stocks or bonds during the year at a profit. This is called realized capital gains. These are also paid out to the shareholders, usually once or twice a year.

3. The fund may hold stocks or bonds that appreciate in value. This is referred to as unrealized capital gains. If the fund holds onto appreciated securities, the value of the fund increases.

Fund Share Valuation

Who determines the value of your shares in a fund? Moody Mr. Market does, of course. Let's start a brand-new fund, called the Frugal Fund, to use as an example.

On its first day of business, the Frugal Fund (we'll call it FFX for short) takes in $100 from Fred Farns, FFX's first investor. Assume that Fred buys all the shares of the fund. The fund arbitrarily sets the value of the shares at $10 per share, so Fred receives 10 shares worth $10 apiece and the fund receives $100. So far, so good.

On the second day of operations, FFX buys four shares of Farmer Fran's Fat Franks—a company supplying hot dogs to supermarket chains—for $25 apiece. The value of the assets owned by FFX is still $100. Fred still owns 10 shares of FFX worth $10 apiece.

Day three is heaven-sent. Farmer Fran's lands a huge contract with three large supermarkets. Income is expected to double! Other investors want to own a piece of Farmer Fran's because of the expected increase in income. The shares of Farmer Fran's Fat Franks are bid up to $30 per share.

FFX still owns four shares, but the value has gone up to $30 per share, so the total value of the assets in the fund is now $120.

Fred Farns, the lucky investor in FFX, still has all 10 shares of the fund, but what are they worth now? The value of the assets owned by FFX is $120, and FFX has a total of 10 shares outstanding: $120 divided by 10 shares equals $12 per share. So each share of FFX is worth $12—and Fred Farns paid $10 per share.

This is an illustration of a process called *marking to market*. Federal regulations require that every fund carry this process out daily so investors know the true value of their shares in the fund.

What Protection Do You Have as an Investor in Funds?

You have no protection from market fluctuation of the shares held within the fund. Remember, it's your job to manage market fluctuation. Your fund manager and/or broker usually won't, but you do have protection from some events.

For example, some people worry that fund managers can either abscond with their assets or make unauthorized investments. Neither can happen because the fund manager doesn't actually have your money. Your money is held in trust at another financial institution. When you send the fund your investment, the money actually goes to this third-party financial institution. When the fund manager wants to invest in Farmer Fran's Fat Franks, she calls the trustee at the financial institution and requests that they buy shares in Farmer Fran's. The trustee checks the bylaws of the fund's operation (known as the fund prospectus) to determine if it's within their power to buy shares of a company such as Farmer Fran's. If so, the trustee makes the investment. If not, the trustee does not.

So the fund does make the investment in Farmer Fran's and the manager feels really good about herself because the shares go up in value so fast. The manager then calls the trustee and says, "You know what? We did so well, I think you should send me $80,000 so I can buy a new Jaguar to reward myself!"

Again, the trustee consults the prospectus. The prospectus spells out exactly how the managers are compensated, and if there's nothing in the prospectus about Jaguar bonuses, the trustee won't send her the money and the manager is confined to her Pinto.

This is why investors are always encouraged to consult the prospectus before investing in funds. The prospectus is an agreement spelling out exactly what you can expect from the fund and what the fund can expect from you.

The Costs of Running a Fund

It costs money to run any business and the mutual fund business is no exception. Funds make money in a number of ways.

First, all funds charge investors on an ongoing basis. This is referred to as *expense ratio*, which helps pay for the fund's managers, lawyers, accountants, printers, clerks, receptionist, client service, etc. Also, some funds charge a distribution, or 12b-1, fee, which is used to cover various marketing costs. All these expenses are expressed as a percentage of a fund's net assets.

You don't need to worry about the minutia. The expense ratio is a combination of all the expenses associated with your fund (other than the sales charge or load), so it's easy for you to compare funds. Also, keep in mind that when you see the performance figures for a fund, those figures are shown *net* of all expenses. Such fees are sometimes reasonable and often not, and they vary from fund to fund.

What Is a Load Fund?

Some funds also make money on a one-time basis on top of their ongoing expense ratio fees. This is referred to as load, and it refers to the commission you're charged for the privilege of allowing the fund to manage your money.

There are three kinds of load funds. Most load mutual fund companies offer each of their funds in the A, B, or C share variety. The funds are almost identical in terms of portfolio and management style; the big difference between them is the fee structure.

A shares have a front-end load, meaning you pay a commission that's taken off the top of what you invest on the day you invest. This commission could be as high as 5.5 percent of the money you invest.

As the amount you invest goes up, the commission declines. For example, if you invest only $25,000, your commission might be 5.5 percent, but if you invest $100,000, that commission might drop to 4 percent. When you sell your A shares, you don't pay any redemption fees.

B shares charge a back-end load. If you sell the shares and withdraw the money from the fund family prior to the maturity date, you pay a sales charge. The maturity date of B shares ranges from five to seven years. In the first few years, the sales charge may be as high as 5 percent and then the fee is reduced each year. In the final year, you pay no sales charge if you withdraw the money. Some investors think that if you hold these B share funds long enough, you don't pay anything. Are they right? No, they're wrong. Every fund in the galaxy has expenses, as mentioned earlier. The B shares have much higher ongoing management fees than A shares. It wouldn't be unheard of for a B share to charge investors more than 3 percent a year in management fees—and 3 percent of $100,000 is $3,000—*every year!*

Enter the world of C shares, if you dare. These shares don't charge you up front and they don't have a long surrender period. In most cases, you have to keep your money in C shares for only one year or 18 months to avoid paying commissions. But the management fees for these funds are usually as high or higher than the astronomical fees of B shares. The table on page 201 summarizes the ongoing management fee structure for two different funds and each of their three fee structures. These are real and very popular funds but I've omitted the name of the fund family.

As you can see, if you invest $100,000 in the New Opportunities A shares, you pay .98 percent or $980 each year in expenses. If you buy the B or C shares, you pay $1,730 a year.

	Fund Expense
New Opp A	0.98
New Opp B	1.73
New Opp C	1.73
Basic Value A	0.56
Basic Value B	1.58
Basic Value C	1.58

What do these numbers mean to you as an investor? If you put your $100,000 into the New Opportunities B fund, you pay an extra $750 every year for management, even though it's managed approximately the same way as the lesser expensive Class A fund. These high fees: (a) explain why mutual funds push investors to buy and hold, (b) allow your broker to make money and play golf at the same time, and (c) cost you a fortune because they dupe you into buying and holding.

No-Load Funds

As their name implies, no-load funds don't charge you a commission to buy or sell the fund. Like all funds, they have ongoing management fees. These fees could be either very low or very high—just because a fund is no-load doesn't mean it's appropriate for you or that it's the least expensive alternative.

How do you determine what fees your funds charge? The details of all fund fees are buried in the prospectus. You can call the fund company to request a prospectus even if you don't own the fund.

Another way to learn about fund fees is to research the fund with a Morningstar report. You can obtain these reports at the public library or through the Internet. Unfortunately, very few people read the prospectus or take the time to understand the fees their funds charge. As a result, most investors never know how expensive the funds they own are. For a free report on your mutual fund, go to www.NealFrankle.com.

About the Author

Neal Frankle has been assisting senior investors for nearly twenty years. He started his career as an accountant with a large aerospace company and moved into advising individuals as vice-president of investments at Great Western Financial Securities and then American Savings Bank Financial Services.

In 1990, the leading magazine for the bank brokerage industry selected Neal as one of the Ten Outstanding Investment Brokers in the United States based on his outstanding client service.

He has been certified by various educational and regulatory organizations for professional services, including designation as a Certified Financial Planner® professional, Certified Senior Advisor, and Registered Investment Advisor.

Neal lives in southern California with his family: wife Mimi and daughters Rinat, Mor, and Maya.

Learn more about Neal and his financial services at www.NealFrankle.com. You can also send an e-mail message to him at Neal@NealFrankle.com.

Printed in the United States
19052LVS00001B/127-174